The Relentless Pursuit of Excellence for CHRIST

Robert Leslie Holmes

The Relentless Pursuit
of
Excellence for Christ

FIRST PRESS
320 Sixth Avenue, Pittsburgh, Pennsylvania 15222

ISBN: 0-9657502-1-3

Printed in the United States of America by Morris Publishing
3212 E. Hwy 30, Kearney, NE 68847

Scripture references not otherwise identified are from
the HOLY BIBLE. NEW INTERNATIONAL VERSION.
Copyright 1973, 1978, 1984 by International Bible Society.
Used by permission of Zondervan Publishing House.

To

The Session of the First Presbyterian Church of Pittsburgh
whose prayers and commitment to Christ helped frame the dream
that forms the outline of this book
and whose dedication to Christ is a wonderful source of
encouragement for this pastor and our people;
and to
The People of our Church
who have already demonstrated their commitment to Christ and to
the dream in magnificent ways;
and especially to
Barbara
a loyal partner in life and in ministry who has been a source of
grace, wisdom and encouragement
and who has helped many of my dreams come true;
this book is dedicated with affection and gratitude

To Sidney Gilmore,
with prayers for God's
blessings — Jim Holmes
Proverbs 3:5-6

Preface

Excellence, said Booker T. Washington, is to do ordinary things in an extraordinary way. He was right, of course.

That is the foundational message of this book. In late 1996 the Elders of the historic First Presbyterian Church of Pittsburgh met together at our Ligonier Camp and Conference Center. We gathered to pray together and to design a new Mission Statement that would be our standard for doing Christ's work into the 21st Century. It was one of the most amazing retreats I have attended in over twenty-five years of pastoral ministry. God's Spirit met us with power and the result was the Mission Statement referred to throughout this book.

In preparing these messages for publication I have had two goals in mind. First, that they might serve as an inspiring resource for our church family and new members who come to join us; and second, that they might be a source of encouragement for ordinary people who in their own lives desire to pursue excellence for Him who loved us all the way to Calvary. If they achieve these goals then I am more than amply rewarded.

I dare not leave the reader with the idea that this is a one man effort. The entire congregation of Pittsburgh's First Presbyterian Church through their grace and generosity made a contribution to this volume. Without the help of my staff, especially Betty Chapman, Douglas Dunderdale and Bob Fletcher who made it possible for me to devote the time necessary to bring this project to completion it would have never been accomplished. Particular members of our church family stepped forward to encourage the initial printing and I am more grateful to them than words can express; especially helpful in this regard was Debra Krumenacker.

Our dear friend, Amy Browning, allowed us to use her home as a retreat where in quietness and peace most of the final work for this little volume could be completed. We owe Amy a debt of gratitude for this and much, much more. My wife, Barbara, not only sacrificed a significant part of her vacation (in San Francisco, her favorite city, of all places) in order that I could give attention to refining this project, she read each chapter and made suggestions that were adopted in each one. For her and to her there will always be due a special measure of love and gratitude.

Jesus used parables constantly in His earthly ministry and no preacher can adequately tell Christ's story without illustrations. So far as is possible I have tried to give credit where I have known the source of my stories. If I have unwittingly quoted someone without giving proper credit please accept my apology and be assured that where I am notified proper credit will be given in any future editions of this work.

My prayer as I send this volume forth is that God will be pleased to use it to inspire our people to great new heights of excellence for His glory and to turn lives in the relentless pursuit of excellence for Christ wherever it goes.

Soli Deo Gloria!

Robert Leslie Holmes
Summer 1997

The Relentless Pursuit of Excellence for Christ

The Mission Statement
of
The First Presbyterian Church of Pittsburgh

"Jesus Christ is the same yesterday and today and forever"
(Hebrews 13:8).

We, the First Presbyterian Church of Pittsburgh, stand
steadfastly for:
- Our Foundation: The Bible, God's Word;
- Our Lord: Jesus Christ, God's only Son;
- Our highest priority: To proclaim Christ's cross and
resurrection and demonstrate His love;
- Our highest goal: That all may know the saving power
of the gospel and live a life worthy of Christ's calling;
- Our strength: The Holy Spirit

Contents

Chapter

1

Our Cornerstone: Jesus Christ!

Keep on loving each other as brothers. Do not forget to entertain strangers, for by so doing some people have entertained angels without knowing it. Remember those in prison as if you were their fellow prisoners, and those who are mistreated as if you yourselves were suffering. Marriage should be honored by all, and the marriage bed kept pure, for God will judge the adulterer and all the sexually immoral. Keep your lives free from the love of money and be content with what you have, because God has said, "Never will I leave you; never will I forsake you." So we say with confidence, "The Lord is my helper; I will not be afraid. What can man do to me?" Remember your leaders, who spoke the word of God to you. Consider the outcome of their way of life and imitate their faith. Jesus Christ is the same yesterday and today and forever.

--Hebrews 13:1-8

The *Christian Century* magazine for November 6, 1996, carried this advertisement: "SENIOR MINISTER—Berkeley CA church seeks minister for local non-denominational congregation. Position open to Christians and non-Christians."

The closing sentence of that advertisement serves as an indicator for how far astray we have drifted in America in our mad quest for theological relativism. Many people are looking for a god (small "g") to meet their mood of the moment and who has no preset opinions or rules that stand in the way of their own designs on life.

A plethora of new religious ideologies are presented to meet this shallow spiritual yen.

Add to this the fact that we live in days of overwhelming change. You probably do not need to be reminded of that. It matters not where you live or work you see the evidence of it all around you. When I spoke not long ago at Grove City College the president of that institution told me of a program which puts a new notebook computer in the hands of every entering freshman student. He reported how in one order for about two thousand computers there were three upgrades even though the same model number was listed on the invoice. Imagine, three times in that one shipment specifications were advanced. That is an indicator of how rapidly change is taking place in some parts of our world. Many of you know about change first hand. Not only computerization but foreign competition and corporate mergers have been calling, and will increasingly call, us to adjust the way we live.

Our New Mission Statement

It was against this backdrop that some of our elders recently encouraged me to write the foundation for a new Mission Statement for our church. What is a Mission Statement, some of you may be asking. The answer is that a Mission Statement is a succinct declaration of why we exist. My initial expression of a new Mission Statement for First Presbyterian Church of Pittsburgh was presented to our leaders during a Fall retreat at Ligonier Camp and Conference Center. There our elders received it for changes and adoption. A copy of the final product was published in our bulletins and newsletters over the next several months. You will find your copy at the beginning of this book and reconstructed phrase by phrase in each chapter.

As I prayerfully contemplated my assignment, these words from Hebrews chapter 13 returned again and again to the forefront of my thinking: *"Jesus Christ is the same yesterday and today and forever."* If like me you find some change uncomfortable, I hope you will be encouraged again by what they affirm. They are the cornerstone of everything else in our Mission Statement.

"Jesus Christ is the same yesterday and today and forever." What is this Bible declaration asserting? And, how does it instruct us? In this age of perpetual change it says that there is Someone with whom we can have a very personal relationship, both as a church and individually, who does not change. That Someone is Jesus Christ our Lord.

We Change But He Is the Same

Our personality and other important factors about our character constantly evolve. Time changes us. Your portrait from years ago hangs on a wall in your home. It vividly tells the story of change. Every time we apply for a new passport the United States Government requests a new photograph. Why? The Passport Agency of our government has observed that the ten years between the issuance of one passport and the next one can bring significant changes to how we look. Sometimes the change is more evident than at others. For example, the picture on a baby's passport is dramatically different from the one sealed in the passport for that child when he or she is ten years old. On the other hand, the change in our mid years may not be quite so sensational but it is there nevertheless.

As we reach life's later years, changes often accelerate again. The eye which once flashed with fire is perhaps dimmed with many tears or now surrounded by bifocals. Hair once plentiful and radiant red is now scarce and gray. Face, form, and gait, all testify to change. There is a far more telling portrait, or should be. The mental portrait, could it be seen, would display opinions altered through new learning and experiences. Priorities change and temperaments are softened against the hard experiences that often come into our lives for our good even though we may not realize it at the time. They change the way we look at life, or even simply how we look. Affections cool too. Early life passions for people, places and experiences often modify with time. Time does that for us; but time has no impact on the eternal Jesus.

It does not take years for change to occur in us. Moods can transform our personality in an instant. We all know people who are like sweet peas one day and lemons the next. If you want to get along with them you must first come just close enough to see what the mood of the day is. That is never so with Jesus. He is never tired, never inconvenienced, irritable, never moody. He is always the same.

Circumstances and experiences change us. Joseph, the son of Jacob, learned the hard way that a butler in prison will promise any favor but will promptly forget back in the palace portico. Similarly, new power or wealth can alter us amazingly. Someone who in lack and obscurity was approachable and genial becomes tyrannical and arrogant in affluence and ascendancy. Not Jesus, however! *"He did not consider equality with God something to be grasped, but..humbled himself and became obedient to death—even death on a cross!" (Philippians 2:6-9).* He was the same Lord in heaven's throne-room as He was on Jerusalem's streets and Calvary's cross. Nothing will ever change Him.

Sin changes us. It makes us either better or bitter. It softens our hearts through the acknowledgment of wrong or hardens them through an unwillingness to repent. Peter was bitter, you remember; but only because he had not experienced first-hand Christ's amazing willingness to love, forgive, and renew him. Peter's problem was not that Christ had not forgiven him but that he had not forgiven himself. Three times Jesus asked him, *"Do you love me?"*

14

Three times Peter tried his best to answer the question but his best was not good enough. It was the loving Lord's way of making Peter face his own inadequacy and Christ's all sufficient grace. He was demonstrating that Peter's love may at times be fickle but His own love for Peter would always be invariable.

Today He comes to us with the same question. He is not oblivious to our sins. His eye has followed us into each wayward wandering. He is a first person witness to the change it brought over us and in us by each of life's experiences whether good or bad. We have been changed but He has not. He still asks: *"Do you love Me?"* No matter what our answer, He still loves us with the amazing love He alone can give. Our sins can no more change His heart towards us than Roman nails could keep Him on a cross.

His message is still, "Behold! I stand at the door and knock. If anyone hears my voice and opens the door, I will come in and eat with him, and he with me" (Revelation 3:20). Today His knock is constant. The only inconstant is how we shall answer. He never changes.

Therefore, He alone is the Cornerstone of our existence at First Presbyterian Church of Pittsburgh.

Our Unfailing Lord!

"Jesus Christ is the same yesterday and today and forever." Other religious systems and philosophies, and life itself, will change and pass, but Christ will always be the same. The splendid gothic building commonly called, "First Presbyterian Church of Pittsburgh" and in which we meet changes. As a matter of fact, this is the fourth "First Church" building in Pittsburgh. The first three buildings were in a different location. The first was a log cabin church built to bear witness to Jesus Christ and meet the needs of our earliest congregation. The second building was constructed of red bricks and was larger to meet the ministry

15

needs of a growing congregation and city and the third was built with gray stone and was larger again than the second. All three of those buildings stood facing Wood Street. A study of old Pittsburgh photographs at the Heinz Museum quickly demonstrates how our city has always been a place of transition too and it was appropriate that a church with the city in its heart should change to meet the changing needs of its environment. Our city and its buildings have changed and our church edifice has changed with them. Our address is different but our Lord is always the same, *"Yesterday and today and forever."* In Francis Shaeffer's words, "He is always there."

One of the ways God demonstrates His continuing love for us is by sending new disciples with an expanding array of talents to serve Christ among us. Just as our buildings have changed, so also the faces in our church pews and figures in our pulpits and Sunday School classrooms have changed. Little children have been baptized, grown to adulthood and been married here. Some have graduated from among us to the Church Triumphant. New programs have been introduced and old ones have died or been revitalized to meet the changing needs of the city we serve, but the Lord of this part of Christ's Church is constant. He is the only member of First Presbyterian Church of Pittsburgh no longer subject to death. He is our Captain. He has been. He still is. He will be. This is our pledge to Him and to each other and so we make it our cornerstone.

He unites seed and egg for our children at conception and wakes them to life on earth at birth. He seals them to Himself in baptism, and saves them to Himself in conversion. He nurtures them to Himself through sanctification, restores them to Himself when they fail, raises them to Himself when they are knocked down. He feeds us, warms us, and loves us until that day when the last of us join the first of us on that shore where there is no sunset and no shadow.

When we are slow to act, He is slow to anger. When we look dirty with sin, He sees past the dirt to our potential, and washes us off with His blood shed once for all time on Calvary. There will come no day for us; not tomorrow, not this year and not next year, not ever, when we will wake up without His love. There is no graveside where He is not present and no burden too big for His shoulders to bear.

All He Was, He Is; All He Is, He Will Be!

This Jesus who never changes is in the business of transforming lives. We believe His miracle working power still transforms people for the better. That is why we exist in His name. Do you know Him as your personal Lord and Savior? I hope so. If you do not, then I invite you to ask Him into your heart now. Simply pray quietly where you are as you read this, "Lord Jesus Christ, I ask you to forgive my sins and invite you into my life from this day forward. All I am and have is yours for now and forever. Amen."

When we pray that prayer or one like it, Christ comes into our lives and begins to transform us into better people. Receive Him today and you will never again be alone or groping in the dark for life's meaning. Seek not a guide, a leader, nor a husband for your soul. You have the Son of eternity within your heart. All He ever was, He is; and all He is, He will always be. Our Cornerstone, *"Jesus Christ is the same yesterday and today and forever."*

Chapter

2

Our Foundation: The Bible, God's Word

While I was with them, I protected them and kept them safe by that name you gave me. None has been lost except the one doomed to destruction so that Scripture would be fulfilled. I am coming to you now, but I say these things while I am still in the world, so that they may have the full measure of my joy within them. I have given them your word and the world has hated them, for they are not of the world any more than I am of the world. My prayer is not that you take them out of the world but that you protect them from the evil one. They are not of the world, even as I am not of it. Sanctify them by the truth; your word is truth.

--John 17:12-17

All Scripture is God-breathed and is useful for teaching, rebuking, correcting and training in righteousness, so that the man of God may be thoroughly equipped for every good work.

--2 Timothy 3:16-17

In His great High Priestly Prayer on the night before His trial and crucifixion, Jesus prays for us to be *"Sanctified by the truth"* then adds these words, *"Your word is truth."* This is our Lord's final great affirmation that God's word has the power to change our lives for the better. Our Mission Statement begins by laying a cornerstone saying that *"Jesus Christ is the same yesterday and today and forever."* Following that, the first firm declaration we make is that the Bible, God's word, is the foundation on which our life together stands.

"We, the First Presbyterian Church of Pittsburgh, stand steadfastly for:

Our Foundation......the Bible, God's Word."

What do we mean by that? We mean that we hold the Bible to be God's infallible, inerrant word and the foundation for everything we do and try to be. The Bible alone shall be the book of our pulpit, our Sunday School and the various arms of ministry in which our church is involved for Christ's sake. This belief in the high authority of Scripture is a distinctive that will set us apart from many other fellowships or congregations. We live, as was written in the last chapter, in a world of theological relativism. Theological relativism, often called "The New Age," puts its emphasis on excessive individuality. It says that our first goal is to be true to ourselves. Translated into the vernacular of our day it declares that the Bible is only true if I decide it is true for me. Similarly, only that part is true which I have decided is true for me. Therefore, if I believe that some parts of the Bible are true and some parts are not true that is all right.

At First Presbyterian Church of Pittsburgh we teach and believe that truth is true whether it is believed or not. Truth does not depend upon popular acceptance to be true. Truth is absolute. It stands alone. When we declare the Bible to be God's infallible and inerrant word and true in all its parts, that declaration at once leads us to what philosophy calls the epistemological question.

Epistemology is that division of philosophy and learning that investigates the nature and origin of knowledge. How do we know

what we know? How do you know, for example, that 2 plus 2
equals 4? How do we know that the Bible is God's inspired word?
A well produced, current television commercial sets the *Book of
Mormon*, on a par with the Bible. How do we know that the Bible is
the word of God and the Book of Mormon is not?

The Testimony Of The Bible

We know first of all because the Bible repeatedly claims to be
God's revealed word and no credible witness has ever successfully
refuted that claim. Most of the scriptures of the other great
religions never make such a claim for themselves. Buddha, for
example, never claims that his writings are divine revelation,
neither does Confucius. Against that, over two thousand times the
Old Testament alone claims: *"This is what the Lord said...The word
of the Lord came to...God said."* How do we know that the Bible is
God's unique word? The Bible self-attests that it is and when it
makes such a declaration it puts its own credibility on the line. We
declare by means of our Mission Statement that we believe what
the Bible says.

Not only Old Testament writers say God's word is inspired, New
Testament authors also repeatedly attribute God's inspiration for
their writing. None is any more determined to make this point than
the apostle Paul who tells young preacher Timothy, *"All Scripture
is God-breathed."*

In doing so, Paul makes a sturdy assertion and coins a powerful
new Greek word. His assertion comes in the form of the word,
"All." The word Paul uses means there are no exceptions to the
statement he is about to make. His new word is actually a
compound of two Greek words. The word is *theopneustos*, from
Theos for God, plus *pneustos* (from which we get our word
pneumatic) for breath. In a sense then Paul is not only saying that
God inspired the Scriptures but that he actually breathed them out

20

through the hands of human authors. That is to say that the Holy Spirit allowed the writers to use their own styles, personalities, and figures of speech while sealing the accuracy of the message they wrote. So we conclude that the Bible is God's word given through chosen, guarded personalities for us.

The Testimony Of The Prophets

After the testimony of the Bible itself there is also the testimony of the prophets, who wrote in advance of events actually happening. Whole books are written on this subject. Think about just a few Bible prophecies concerning the birth of Jesus:

Over seven hundred years before Christ was born, the prophet Isaiah said that John the Baptizer would be Christ's forerunner and that Jesus would be born of a virgin mother (see *Isaiah 40:3* and *Isaiah 7:14*). About the same time, the prophet Micah testified with incredible accuracy that Jesus would be born in a tiny hamlet called Bethlehem (see *Micah 5:2*). The Book of Psalms, written between approximately 1440 and 586 years before Jesus was born, is filled with prophecies about His life, death and message. *Psalm 22*, for example, predicted He would die on a cross and that evil men would cast lots for His clothes, and *Psalm 16:8-10* says He would rise again from the dead. The stunning accuracy with which these and many other prophecies speak about our Savior hundreds of years before He was born stand as proof positive that He is truly the Messiah of God and that no ordinary hand guided the pen that wrote the book we call the Holy Bible.

Consider against this that the only prophecy in the Koran, Islam's holy book, is one Mohammed proposed to control himself: He said that he would return to Mecca. Jesus, Lord of the cross, on the other hand, prophesied He would return from the dead, and, of course, He did!

Bible prophecies are not, of course, restricted to Christ alone or even to people. There are amazing prophecies about places. Take, for example, the City of Nineveh, capital of the historic Assyrian Empire. Nineveh ruled the world of its day. When Nineveh was at its peak Nahum prophesied, *"The LORD has given a command concerning you, Nineveh: 'You will have no descendants to bear your name. I will destroy the carved images and cast idols that are in the temple of your gods. I will prepare your grave, for you are vile'"* (Nahum 1:14).

Nineveh's egotistical pagan scholars laughed in Nahum's face. They foolishly believed that Nineveh was indestructible. What happened? Edward Gibbon writing in *The Rise and Fall of the Roman Empire* describes the destruction of Nineveh in ways that parallel Nahum's words completely. This is perhaps especially remarkable inasmuch as Edward Gibbon was a self-professing skeptic when it came to religion.

I read not long ago that modern Atlanta, the capital city of the New South, is growing faster than any region in world history. After Nineveh fell from prominence Babylon, modern Baghdad, rose to power. Babylon was probably the greatest city ever built. Totally self-sufficient, Babylon had a balance of trade unequaled in history. Babylon needed to import nothing. It was the kind of situation politicians and economists dream about.

Babylon's citizens were intelligent. Our little granddaughters, Hannah and Cameron sing a song about learning their "ABC's." The first lesson in learning any language is learning the alphabet of that language. Long before there was an English language, Babylonians saw the need for writing down language in a universal way and gave civilization the first-ever alphabetized language.

Do modern computers impress you? They do me. Babylonian scholars solved the first math problems. Had Babylonians not given us that foundation, computers might never have been developed. Look at the time on your watch. Babylonians first saw the value of measuring time and invented clocks to keep up with it.

As I write these words during my Summer vacation, I can look out of a window across from my desk and survey San Francisco's fascinating skyline. Not far away is the world famous Transamerica Building with its lofty pointed tower reaching towards the heavens. From what I have observed, it seems that every one of these buildings is finished in concrete. Babylonians first saw the value of baking clay into concrete blocks for construction purposes. Before Babylon rose to prominence, builders in other societies regarded clay as nothing more than muck. They considered it useless as a building material except for the most temporary of buildings. The Babylonians were the first great students of science. Today almost every branch of the scientific world can trace its roots to ancient Babylon.

We have all seen television photographs of China's Great Wall. The Babylonians constructed a larger, stronger, and more impenetrable wall than China's wall thousands of years before Chinese architects drew up their plans. It was as wide as some parts of the American Interstate system, designed so that four chariots could be driven side-by-side around its perimeter. The Babylonians were very proud of it. By way of intimidating contrast, Babylon scorned Jerusalem's walls as tiny by comparison and threatened to break down the walls and crush Jerusalem. Isaiah, in turn, called Babylon, *"The jewel of kingdoms" (Isaiah 13:19)* and forecast a Babylonian doom equal to Sodom and Gomorrah if Babylon ever attempted to carry out that threat. The brilliant Babylonian warlords mocked him. Saying Isaiah was a nobody they sneered about him being deluded. Ego convinced them they would be the leading city of the world for all time. But, *"Those who walk in pride God is able to humble" (Daniel 4:37)*. In God's perfect timing, Isaiah's words came true and Babylon's walls fell like the Iron Curtain that divided Europe for almost fifty years after World War II.

Jerusalem's city walls, on the other hand, still stand. I have walked across them. God, through Isaiah (see *Isaiah 33:20*), Jeremiah (see *Jeremiah 39:8*), Daniel (see *Daniel 9:25*), and Micah (see *Micah 7:11*) foretold Babylon's future of troublesome times and tyrannical leaders. What is happening in Babylon today? Saddam Hussein rules as the latest in a line of despots. That should not surprise us. God's word said it would be so.

The Testimony Of The Lord
Our Lord Jesus Christ was committed to the authority of the Scriptures. *"It is written,"* He replied every time Satan tempted Him. For the Lord what the Scriptures said was enough and it settled a matter conclusively. When the religious leaders of His day challenged Him, He pointed out that they were failing to understand their own holy writings: *"You diligently study the Scriptures because you think that by them you possess eternal life. These are the Scriptures that testify about me, yet you refuse to come to me to have life" (John 5:39,40)*. That Christ held the Scriptures to be trustworthy and recognized their authority is an absolute and undeniable fact. That alone should sufficiently inspire all who claim to be His disciples to study God's word.

Yet, the Scriptures tell us even more about the Lord Jesus than that He had confidence in them. They also demonstrate how far He was willing to go to redeem us. You can search the world over and read every book ever written but you will never find another book like the book that first told humanity about God's love in Jesus.

24

God's Incredible Book

Think about it: Here is a book written by assorted writers from unrelated backgrounds who speak various languages and diverse dialects. They include a king, physician, herdsman, tax collector, theologian, scribe, and fisherman. In a time before the Internet and FAX, when communication was virtually non-existent, it is likely many of them had no idea the others even existed. In that diversity there was not much hope for collusion or communication. Forty different writers spread over sixty-four generations produced sixty-six books with the complete harmony and precision of a well-made jigsaw puzzle. Together they tell us everything we need to know about God who made all things. They promise that God will meet us in our every need and heal our every hurt. They inspire us in our lowliness, accompany us in our loneliness, strengthen us in our weakness, and bring us through our dark nights into bright new tomorrow's. There is a positive word of encouragement for every decision we shall ever face. Above all else, this book speaks plainly about God's love for us in Jesus, His Son. It has no equal. How else would we explain this book except to say that it comes to us by the hand of God?

So, our Mission Statement declares for all the world to see that we are a people of one book and our book is the Bible, the word of God written for us. God's great book is about Jesus meeting you and me at the point of our deepest need. This book is our foundation because we all need a foundation on which to build our lives and our life together.

You also need a firm foundation on which to build a life worth living. Come and join us in this mission we walk in together in Him.

25

Chapter

3

Our Lord, Jesus Christ, God's Only Son!

He is the image of the invisible God, the firstborn over all creation.
For by him all things were created: things in heaven and on earth,
visible and invisible, whether thrones or powers or rulers or
authorities; all things were created by him and for him. He is before
all things, and in him all things hold together. And he is the head of
the body, the church; he is the beginning and the firstborn from
among the dead, so that in everything he might have the supremacy.
For God was pleased to have all his fullness dwell in him, and
through him to reconcile to himself all things, whether things on
earth or things in heaven, by making peace through his blood, shed
on the cross. Once you were alienated from God and were enemies in
your minds because of your evil behavior. But now he has reconciled
you by Christ's physical body through death to present you holy in
his sight, without blemish and free from accusation-- if you continue
in your faith, established and firm, not moved from the hope held
out in the gospel. This is the gospel that you heard and that has been
proclaimed to every creature under heaven, and of which I, Paul,
have become a servant.

--Colossians 1:15-23

Colossae, a multicultural city, was 125 miles Southeast of
Ephesus on the way to Rome. The population was principally
composed of immigrants from Greece, Rome and Israel. As far as
we know the apostle Paul never visited there. His influence was felt

among the Christians in Colossae, however, primarily because of stories travelers to Colossae told about Paul's ministry in Ephesus.

When Billy Graham preached at Three Rivers Stadium in Pittsburgh my parents, who were visiting from Ireland at the time, attended the meetings. Later they traveled on to Waterloo, Ontario, Canada where they spent time with my sister, Sandra and her family. The next time I was in Waterloo a friend of my sister spoke about my parent's report about Dr. Graham's meetings in Pittsburgh. Paul's relationship with the Colossian Christians was in a similar vein. People who sat under his preaching talked about it wherever their journeys took them from there.

Therefore, when confusion arose in the Colossian church it was no surprise that Epaphras, a Colossian Christian, who perhaps had business in Rome visited Paul in prison there. Epaphras told Paul about new teachings that threatened the purity of the gospel in the Colossian church and asked for Paul's advice. In that context one of the great epistles of the New Testament was born and included in it was the most succinct Christological definition in the entire Bible.

The defective new teaching that was infecting the Colossian church was called Gnosticism. Gnosticism reckoned Christianity to be a purely academic matter. It set knowledge on a higher level of importance than a personal relationship with Christ and even called into question who Jesus was. Compounding that confusion was Gnosticism's stipulation that the old Jewish temple rites and traditions must still be followed. Thus, Gnostic teachers promoted circumcision, dietary laws, and the Jewish feast observances as necessary parts of salvation. They failed to see that Christ alone is all we need to be saved.

That is not as strange a doctrine as it seems at first glance. It recurs in almost every generation in church history. Today it is the core of Jehovah's Witness teaching. It presents a destructive and unhealthy view of the gospel that challenges Christ's deity by saying He is not God but the highest of all created beings, a creature rather than the Creator. Paul's primary purpose in writing his Colossian letter is to refute this notion: *"God was pleased to have all his fullness dwell in him."*

These words are the Bible text for the second pillar of our new Mission Statement:

We, the First Presbyterian Church of Pittsburgh, stand steadfastly for:
> *Our Foundation......the Bible, God's Word;*
> **Our Lord......Jesus Christ, God's only Son.**

In a world of increasing secularization, First Presbyterian Church of Pittsburgh will continue to declare Christ's Lordship over all things. This again brings us face to face with the epistemological question: How do we know that Jesus Christ, God's Son, is Lord.

We Know Because He Tells Us
Throughout His sermons and teachings Jesus repeatedly claims attributes and powers which are God's alone. He asserts His pre-existence: *"Before Abraham was born, I am!" (John 8:58).* He declares His Omnipotence: *"All authority in heaven and on earth has been given to me" (Matthew 28:18).* He says He is infallible: *"Heaven and earth will pass away, but my words will never pass away" (Mark 13:31).* He promises His Omnipresence: *"I am with you always" (Matthew 28:20).* He maintains personal moral perfection: *"Can any of you prove me guilty of sin?" (John 8:46).* He advances His right to judge: *"The Father judges no one, but has entrusted all judgment to the Son" (John 5:22).* He professes His

28

power to forgive sins: *"Friend, your sins are forgiven" (Luke 5:20).* Finally, in an act which if at all untrue would be absolute blasphemy, He asserts total equality with God: *"I and the Father are one" (John 10:31).* In all these ways, and many more, Jesus Christ claimed to be God. In one of the most pointed declarations of all literature, Christ even went so far as to declare that He alone was the way to God: *"I am the way and the truth and the life. No one comes to the Father except through me" (John 14:6).*

Lunatic? Liar? Lord!

When Christ makes these claims for Himself there are finally only three possible conclusions we can draw. The first is that He was deluded by visions of grandeur. If that is the case we must declare Him a lunatic. The second is that He was perpetrating what has become the greatest confidence scheme ever perpetrated on the human race, in which case let us declare Him a liar without equal. The third is that He is indeed everything He claims to be and we must surrender our lives completely to Him. We at First Presbyterian Church of Pittsburgh are committed to the third of these options. We believe Christ to be all He ever claimed to be and gladly surrender our lives to His service.

Three Great Miracles!

Furthermore, we know that Jesus is Lord because of three great miracles Scripture connects to His life. First, He was born of a virgin just as the prophet Isaiah said He would be: *"The Lord himself will give you a sign: The virgin will be with child and will give birth to a son" (Isaiah 7:14)* and as Matthew confirms (*see Matthew 1:18-25*). Second, He was resurrected from the dead, just as the psalmist David declared He would be: *"I have set the LORD always before me. Because he is at my right hand, I will not be shaken. Therefore my heart is glad and my tongue rejoices; my body also will rest secure, because you will not abandon me to the grave, nor will you let your Holy One see decay" (Psalm 16:8-10)* and as Luke the physician writer of the gospel reports (see *Luke 24:5-7).* Third, He ascended into heaven just as was foretold by David: *"When you ascended on high, you led captives in your train; you received gifts from men, even from the rebellious—that you, O LORD God, might dwell there" (Psalm 68:18)* and as Paul tells us in his Ephesian letter (see *Ephesians 4:8-10).*

The Integrity of His Teachings

We also know that Jesus is Lord because of the integrity of His teachings. In almost 2,000 years no one has improved upon even one of His ethical principles, and no teaching of His has become obsolete. John Stuart Mill, the 20th Century philosopher and scholar asked, "Who among the disciples or their proselytes were capable of inventing the sayings ascribed to Jesus, or imagining the life and character revealed in the Gospel? Certainly not the fishermen of Galilee; and certainly not St. Paul. Still less the early Christian writers, in whom nothing was more evident than that the good that was in them was all derived, as they always confessed, from Him."

The Character Question

One of the most chilling concerns about recent national elections in America is the strong indicator of moral ambivalence they have revealed in our society. Polling data indicates the American public no longer considers character a primary concern for persons in leadership. We seem to be saying that we believe we can expect good leadership from bad people, or people with questionable lifestyle patterns. We are in what Stephen Vincent Bennett calls, "A time with few fixed stars."

Yet, the Bible teaches and history confirms that character means everything in leadership. Just as the old mariners once charted their course across the oceans by studying the stars so even now every life needs "a few fixed stars." That is, we all need something or someone to set our moral compass by. We need life foundations that will not erode in a temporal, fleeting, stressful and uncertain world. No other system of belief stands or falls with the character of its founder like Christianity.

Do you know how you could destroy First Presbyterian Church of Pittsburgh overnight? You could eradicate this church by finding the least flaw in Christ's character. If He has the least fault about Him, He cannot be Lord of the Church He established nor of any particular congregation of it including this one.

For 2,000 years people have dedicated their lives to undermining the good character and moral honor of Jesus Christ. They have included people from almost every scholarly disciple imaginable yet none has ever succeeded in finding a flaw. One of my predecessors, Dr. Clarence Edward MacCartney, in a published sermon titled, *God the Son,* writes, "The very charges which his enemies brought against him were tributes to his character."

That is true. Every time Jesus Christ's enemies charged Him with something it was a half-truth which when the whole truth was told, served not only to vindicate Him but to elevate Him. His enemies said He was a Sabbath-breaker but an investigation of the charge proves that by healing on the Sabbath He put the day in the context God intended. Other adversaries called Him a wine-bibber but when the charge was pursued He was shown to demonstrate hands-on concern for society's down and outs. Other opponents charged that He was in league with the devil but a closer look at His life and at the gospel He left us proves that He broke, and is still breaking, Satan's power over people.

All of these tell us something about who Christ is. Our text challenges us to consider also what Christ has done. During His life on earth and in the almost 2,000 years since He established His church more people have been educated, healed, forgiven and inspired in His name than in all the other names in the history of the world.

Our Advocate

The online edition of my hometown newspaper the *Belfast Telegraph* recently reported a story about a lawyer whose car was stolen. The next day he received a call from a former client who asked the lawyer to defend him against a charge of car theft. Upon further inquiry, the lawyer discovered that the car in question was his car. In a strange turn of events, the victim was hired to defend the thief. When his representation of that client by that attorney was challenged in court the lawyer responded that his client admitted guilt and it was, therefore, perfectly appropriate for him to advocate on behalf of his client.

Let me tell you what the Bible says about Jesus. *"My dear children, I write this to you so that you will not sin. But if anybody does sin, we have one who speaks to the Father in our defense—Jesus Christ, the Righteous One. He is the atoning sacrifice for our sins, and not only for ours but also for the sins of the whole world" (1 John 2:1,2).*

John reaches into the language of the legal world of his day and finds a word declaring that Jesus does more than represent us as our attorney when we do wrong against Him. He took our punishment upon Himself at Calvary's cross, just as Isaiah prophesied He would: *"He was pierced for our transgressions, he was crushed for our iniquities; the punishment that brought us peace was upon him, and by his wounds we are healed" (Isaiah 53:4,5).*

Consider this: Christ Jesus, the One offended by all our sins, not only rushes to our defense, He personally bears the penalty our sins deserve. In so doing, He sets us free from having to suffer it. Amazing as that may seem, it is all the more wondrous that He does all this pro bono, or at no expense to us. What a gracious, generous Lord! The eternal life He offers us costs us nothing even though it cost Him His life.

The Fullness Found in Christ Alone

"For God was pleased to have all his fullness dwell in him." Everything that God is and wants us to be is found in His Son Jesus Christ, the perfect God-man. Jesus is truly God to the fullest extent possible. Nothing God has is lacking in Him. When it comes to humanity, He is the only perfect person who ever lived. The only one who did not need a Savior became our Savior.

All God's fullness found in Christ radiates towards us. Everything you want God to be is found in God's Son Jesus. The ancient godly scholar, Bernard of Clairvoux says it powerfully in his great hymn:

Thou, O Christ, art all I want; All I need in Thee I find.

What This Means For Us

What does this mean for us? It means that because Jesus is all the fullness of God we have a great Redeemer from sin, One whose blood makes us clean. It means we have a firm foundation on which to build our faith. It means that, with Paul, we live by faith in the Son of God who loved us and gave Himself for us (see *Galatians 2:20*). Which brings me at last to personalize this pillar from our church Mission Statement, for this church is, finally, you.

Christ has no hands but ours to do His work. He has no feet but ours to take His ministry to the needy and less fortunate. He has

33

no lips but ours to tell the lost the way to eternal life with Him in His Father's house of many mansions.

Do you believe that Jesus is Lord? What will you give your life to in His service? How will you demonstrate Christ's presence in your life? In this church and in every church that bears His name Christ has high expectations for His people. Each of us is gifted in unique ways for His service. Christ's Reveille trumpet is sounding in your heart as you read these words. Do you hear it? Are you listening? Today and every day He says to each of us, *"I tell you, open your eyes and look at the fields! They are ripe for harvest" (John 4:35).*

Chapter

4

Our Highest Priority:
To Proclaim Christ's Cross ...

Christ did not send me to baptize, but to preach the gospel—not with words of human wisdom, lest the cross of Christ be emptied of its power. For the message of the cross is foolishness to those who are perishing, but to us who are being saved it is the power of God"

--1 Corinthians 1:17-18

Crosses, according to an article in *Vogue* magazine not long ago, are back in style. The high fashion world is promoting a popular revival of cross sales in jewelry stores and fashion boutiques. Crosses have become a definitive fashion accessory of the moment for both men and women. You have no doubt seen them, worn around necks, as ear rings or pinned to jacket lapels by people who are style conscious. Some crosses look very attractive and give evidence of great creativity. I even saw one worn as a finger ring a few days ago. Perhaps you wear one yourself either as a fashion statement or a faith statement.

The Sign of the Cross
Recently a member of our church family stopped by the office to ask if we had a color photograph of the Covenanter church flag.

She was planning to recreate a flag for a history reenactment project and wanted to replicate the flag colors accurately.

Almost every religious system or philosophical ideology in world history has identified itself through the use of some flag or symbol. Ancient Buddhism's lotus flower, for example, depicted the emergence of beauty from the muddy waters of chaos while Islam's crescent symbolizes the Muslim conquest of the old world and intention to capture the new world to its cause. Marxism's hammer and sickle, no longer as popular as once it was, represents the convergence of agriculture and industry through the Industrial Revolution.

The Third Reich's intention was to replace the Christian cross with the Swastika which some people think of as a cross of distorted shape. Adolf Hitler planned for all of Europe's churches to submit to his personal control and direction much as the Communists did in Eastern Europe until not long ago. Point 30 of the National Reich Church Program expressed an intention to replace the Christian cross with the Swastika in every church sanctuary in Europe: "On the day of (the Reich's) foundation, the Christian cross must be removed from all churches, cathedrals and chapels," Nazi leaders wrote. "It must be superseded by the only unconquerable symbol, the Swastika." No wonder the Third Reich lost the war! They unwittingly plotted their own destruction when they wrote those words. History is a commentary on the folly of those who think that somehow they can replace such a primary symbol of Christian faith. Jesus said, *"I will build my church, and the gates of Hades will not overcome it" (Matthew 16:18).*

In Israel of old religious symbols were banned for the Jews. Ancient Judaism rejected visual symbols of its religion out of respect for the second commandment: *"You shall not make for yourself an idol in the form of anything in heaven above or on the earth beneath or in the waters below" (Exodus 20:4).* On a recent trip to Israel, however, it was obvious that things have changed. We saw the Star of David at the center of Israel's national flag hanging on many public buildings and freely available on jewelry and in clothing designs.

In the eighth Century a hearty dispute raged all over Christendom based on the same logic as rule of old Israel. Historians call it the Iconoclastic Controversy. One side said church buildings should bear no symbols lest they themselves become objects of worship while the other argued for a proliferation of symbols to help the people recall the history and primary elements of Christian faith. There are still those within the body of Christ who hold strong views on each side of this subject.

Long before the Iconoclastic Controversy earlier Christians avoided being identified with the cross for fear of being persecuted. For the first generation of believers wearing a cross was looking for trouble. The cross was too readily recognized by those who opposed the gospel. Therefore, for the early disciples the recognized insignia was not a cross but a fish. It was the nearest thing to a universally accepted Christian sign and there was a good reason for that. The Greek word for fish, *ICTHUS*, was an acronym for, "*Iesus Christos, Theou, Huios, Soterios,*" which translates into, "*Jesus Christ, God, Son, Savior!*" That was, in a sense, the first creed of Christ's followers. It was not until the second century that the cross replaced the fish as the principle symbol of the gospel of Jesus Christ. So we rejoice when persons of every religious persuasion, or of no religion, wear a cross for, whether they realize it or not, they bear witness to the price that was paid to redeem us.

The Foolish Cross
"The message of the cross is foolishness to those who are perishing," Paul writes to the Corinthians. Marcus Tullius Cicero, that forceful orator who lived a century before Christ and whose eloquence moved the Roman Senate and helped elevate him among his peers to the highest office in the Roman Republic, said, "The cross speaks of that which is so shameful, so horrible, it should never be mentioned in polite society." He should have known for it was he who led the Roman Senate to adopt the cross as the most heinous way imaginable to demonstrate Rome's power over its subjects.

But the cross does not find its roots in Rome. In ancient Egypt the cross was already a well-known symbol. There it was called a canob, after a T-shaped instrument used to measure the rise and fall of the Nile. As early as 125BC, worshippers of the Greek god Bacchus presented him with flour cakes with the figure of a cross imprinted on them. When Rome rose to prominence as the world's leading power however, the practice of nailing society's worst criminals to a cross in a public place was adopted not only for punishment but as a deterrent against crime.

The cross was the electric chair of its time. It said a person was unfit to live; rejected by humanity and accursed of God. The cross declared that the one hanging on it was not worthy of a place in decent society.

The Ultimate Plus Sign
The apostle Paul, a citizen of Rome, knew all this but after his dramatic conversion on the Damascus Road he was broader minded than Cicero. Paul saw what God had done with Rome's most horrible symbol and wrote, *"May I never boast except in the cross of our Lord Jesus Christ, through which the world has been crucified to me, and I to the world" (Galatians 6:14).*

Cicero, had he lived to see it, would have called Christ's death on the cross an unsurpassed shameful death. Paul, the well educated son of Roman aristocracy, who once would have agreed with Cicero came to regard the cross of Jesus as the only thing he knew worth bragging about. The cross is indeed rough and deadly, but it was above all else effective in accomplishing God's plan for our salvation. That it is worn with pride by leaders in high fashion is wonderful testimony to how God can take a thing of abject disgrace and transform it into something of beauty and splendor. God made the ugly cross of the Romans the world's ultimate plus sign.

It is no wonder then that John Bunyan in his immortal *Pilgrim's Progress* says, "I saw in my dream that just as Christian came up to the cross, his burden loosed from his shoulders and fell from his back and began to tumble till it came to the mouth of the sepulcher, where it fell and I saw it no more. Then was Christian glad and lightsome and said with a merry heart, 'He has given me rest by his sorrow, and life by his death.'"

Dress it up however you like, but it finally comes down to this: That your heart and mine were so putrid in the sight of a holy God that there was no other possible way by which we might be saved. We needed a cross. God took this instrument the world once looked upon with disdain and, through the death of His Son, turned it into an instrument of glory for us.

Already Dead
It is unfortunate that the translators opted for the word, *"perishing,"* in our Scripture text. The original word carries more force than that. It really means abject lostness so that a more realistic translation might read, *"The message of the cross is*

39

foolishness to lost people." The point is that there is a finality about rejecting the cross.

Do you see the difference? Let me illustrate it another way: Paul does not say we are in the process of perishing, that we are on the way to being lost or that we will be lost if we persist in rejecting Christ's cross. He says that outside this cross of Jesus Christ we are already dead and already lost.

The Cross At City Center
At First Presbyterian Church of Pittsburgh we proclaim Christ's cross from the heart of our city without hesitation.

The Scottish poet-preacher George MacLeod perhaps said it best when he wrote:

I simply argue that the cross be raised again at the center of the market place as well as on the steeple of the church,
I am recovering the claim that Jesus was not crucified in a cathedral between two candles;
But on a cross between two thieves on a town garbage heap;
At a crossroad of politics so cosmopolitan that they had to write His title in Hebrew and in Latin and in Greek...
And at the kind of place where cynics talk smut, and thieves curse and soldiers gamble.
Because that is where He died,
And that is what He died about.
And that is where Christ's men ought to be,
And what church people ought to be about.

What George MacLeod expresses about the cross is precisely what we exist for at First Presbyterian Church of Pittsburgh. We believe the Bible teaches that anyone who comes to our services and leaves without a personal relationship with Jesus and a personal understanding of their own need of His cross is a lost person. We know this and so we preach the message of the cross with a high degree of urgency. It is the focal point of everything we do just as our Mission Statement says:

We, the First Presbyterian Church of Pittsburgh, stand steadfastly for:

Our Foundation......the Bible, God's Word;
Our Lord......Jesus Christ, God's only Son;
Our highest priority......to proclaim Christ's cross

In making a statement such as this we recognize that the pseudo-sophistication of our society will cause some people who hear our message of the cross to reject it and we always regret their decision. Some will call us out of touch with our day. This we accept, knowing that we live in an age that often seems to prefer to speak only of God's love and chooses not to remember the desperate final pain God's Son endured on the cross to demonstrate the length to which God's love was willing to go for our sake. We also prefer to speak about God's love but we know that there can be no Easter without Calvary for the cross always comes before the resurrection. When others oppose our message we respectfully but simply revert to Paul's inspired words: *"The message of the cross is foolishness to those who are lost...God was pleased through the foolishness of what was preached to save those who believe" (1 Corinthians 1:21).*

In the cross we find our life and our reason for being. In the cross we find our health and our hope for all eternity. In the cross we find our victories and our protection from our enemies. No powers that earth can imagine could ever separate us from God's love in Christ's cross.

Granny Was Wrong!

An elderly Scots woman went to church regularly most of her life. She always hoped that when she died she would get dying grace and be fit for heaven. One night there were two preachers in the same service. Walking home she met an inquisitive neighbor who asked, "How was church, Granny?"

"We had two preachers tonight," said she.

"Did you like them?"

"Well, I couldn't understand them. One said he was preaching to folk already saved. The people he described were so good I couldn't think of a single soul in our village like that. The other said he was here to speak to people that are lost and he said they are going to hell."

"Which one did you like the best?" the neighbor inquired further.

"Neither one," said Granny, "can you imagine that they had two preachers and neither one had a word for me."

According to Granny's estimation, she was neither lost nor found. Yet, the fact remains that the Bible says there are just two kinds of people in all the world. There are those people who are lost because they reject the message of the cross and those people who are saved because they put full trust in the Christ of Calvary's cross. We want everyone who comes in touch with the ministry of Pittsburgh's First Presbyterian Church to understand this in order that they might make the right decision for Christ's sake.

That means that as you read this you are either a lost person right now, or saved person right now. Which is it? It must be one or the other. Granny was wrong. There was a word for her that evening. Any time the gospel is preached there is always a word for each of us.

If you have never done so before, or if you once did but have somehow drifted away, why not commit or recommit your life to Christ Jesus as you come to the end of this chapter. Take for yourself the message of the cross and you can be sure Christ has saved you. When you receive Him into your life come and join us or join another church where you can take part in lifting high the cross for Christ sake.

Chapter

5

Our Highest Priority:
To Proclaim Christ's...Resurrection

This man was handed over to you by God's set purpose and foreknowledge; and you, with the help of wicked men, put him to death by nailing him to the cross. But God raised him from the dead, freeing him from the agony of death, because it was impossible for death to keep its hold on him. David said about him: "I saw the Lord always before me. Because he is at my right hand, I will not be shaken. Therefore my heart is glad and my tongue rejoices; my body also will live in hope, because you will not abandon me to the grave, nor will you let your Holy One see decay. You have made known to me the paths of life; you will fill me with joy in your presence." Brothers, I can tell you confidently that the patriarch David died and was buried, and his tomb is here to this day. But he was a prophet and knew that God had promised him on oath that he would place one of his descendants on his throne. Seeing what was ahead, he spoke of the resurrection of the Christ, that he was not abandoned to the grave, nor did his body see decay. God has raised this Jesus to life, and we are all witnesses of the fact.

--Acts 2:23-32

After the cross comes the resurrection. Therefore, the phrase we began to look at in chapter four does not end where we last left it but quickly goes on to establish our commitment to Christ overcoming death:

44

We, the First Presbyterian Church of Pittsburgh, stand steadfastly for:

Our Foundation......the Bible, God's Word;
Our Lord......Jesus Christ, God's only Son;
Our highest priority......to proclaim Christ's cross
and resurrection

Christ's Resurrection

The story is often told that Auguste Comte, the French philosopher known as the father of sociology, determined to start a new religion called Positivism. Comte believed that given enough time his new religion would supplant Christianity as the primary religion of Europe. With great enthusiasm, Comte told his friend, the Scottish essayist and student of the French Revolution, Thomas Carlyle of his plans. The sage Carlyle responded, "It sounds like an excellent idea, Comte. All you will need to do will be to speak as no man ever spoke before and live as none has ever been able to live. Next you must be crucified and rise again the third day. If you can do all this and get the world to believe that you are still alive and your being alive again really does inspire people to be better than they were, it will last."

That Jesus Christ died on a Roman cross was the subject of the previous chapter. The Bible says that after His crucifixion Jesus' body was removed from the cross and buried in Joseph of Arimathea's garden tomb. Yet he is no longer there. It was there in that tomb that the greatest miracle in all history occurred. Christ rose again from the dead.

In the forty days following His resurrection Christ appeared on no less than thirteen different occasions and to more than five hundred people. That was the central thrust that set the Christian Church in motion at its beginning. On the day of Pentecost it was the primary point of Peter's sermon when he proclaimed to thousands: *"God raised him from the dead, freeing him from the agony of death, because it was impossible for death to keep its hold on him."*

The Resurrection Fact

Peter's Pentecost sermon consisted of three undeniable points about Jesus' resurrection. There was a declaration, an affirmation and an explanation. The declaration was that *"God raised Him."* That was followed by an affirmation that *"It was impossible for death to keep its hold on Him."* Finally, Peter explained that this was all part of God's eternal plan. He did so by quoting the prophetic words of Psalm 16: *"David said about him: I saw the Lord always before me. Because he is at my right hand, I will not be shaken. Therefore my heart is glad and my tongue rejoices; my body also will live in hope, because you will not abandon me to the grave, nor will you let your Holy One see decay. You have made known to me the paths of life; you will fill me with joy in your presence."*

The resurrection of Jesus from the dead is one of the spiritual foundations of First Presbyterian Church of Pittsburgh. Our present joy and future hope is uniquely connected to it.

Our Resurrection Proclamation

Saying that we proclaim Christ's resurrection is not intended to imply that we know all there is to know about it. We are willing learners in His service. Each of us with Paul the apostle declares, *"I want to know Christ and the power of his resurrection"* *(Philippians 3:10).* Thus we make it our aim to personally experience resurrection power every day in each of our lives and thereby to grow in the knowledge and love of the living Jesus.

Proclaiming Christ's resurrection sets us apart in three ways that affect all of life for us:

Life After Death

First, it declares our belief in life after death. Jesus promised He would go to prepare a place for us, so that we would dwell with Him forever in His Father's house. Death holds no eternal threat for us. We shall rise again, for He said so: *"I am the resurrection and the life. He who believes in me will live, even though he dies"* *(John 11:25)*. *"Before long, the world will not see me anymore, but you will see me. Because I live, you also will live"* *(John 14:19)*.

Only Christ's disciples can claim resurrection power for only Christ has conquered death. Think about it: Confucius' disciples, Buddha's disciples, Mohammed's disciples find their masters' tombs occupied. Death has taken each of them away. The tomb where Jesus once lay dead is vacant, however, for He has taken death away.

Christ's Deity

Second, our resurrection message tells the world we are committed to believe in Christ's deity. We confirm our conviction that all the prophecies and claims made about Him in the Bible are true. There is even more to our resurrection message than immortality. No ordinary mortal could rise from the dead. He who conquered death had to be the Son of the living God. Writing to the Romans Paul says Jesus was, *"Declared with power to be the Son of God by his resurrection from the dead"* *(Romans 1:4)*.

The Victorious Life

Third, because we believe in a living Savior and because we believe that He is God, we believe in His power to bring victory over any situation or circumstance. *"God raised him from the dead, freeing him from the agony of death, because it was impossible for death to keep its hold on him."* Our resurrection message says our Christ declared victory over the grave: *"I am the Living One; I was dead, and behold I am alive for ever and ever!" (Revelation 1:18).* If death could not hold Him nothing can hold Him. If nothing can hold Him we believe nothing can hold those who by grace belong to Him.

Four hundred years before Jesus lived the Greek poet Agathon said, "Even God cannot change the past." Historically speaking, Agathon is right, of course. God never goes back and rewrites history nor does He call us to live yesterday again. The past is gone. Yet when God raised Christ from the dead He provided a way to transform all our yesterdays into foundation stones for a wonderful new beginning. *"I will repay you for the years the locusts have eaten—the great locust and the young locust, the other locusts and the locust swarm" (Joel 2:25).*

Life Over Death

We often hear talk about, "the wasted years" of someone's life. God declares through Joel the prophet that He will make use even of our "wasted years."

There is something about the past in all of us that we wish was not there, but it is. What can we do about it? We can turn it over to God and He will find a way to redeem it in our new life in Him.

When we think back on how we have sometimes reacted in the face of pain, sorrow, ill reproach, trouble, and temptation, we could hang our heads in shame. There are times in my own life when it must have looked as though the Lord I confessed was anemic and insufficient to meet my needs, unable to save Himself, much less me. Yet, the truth is that the weakness came at the point of my faith and not at the point of His power. Even Paul the apostle had to learn this: *"My grace is sufficient for you, for my power is made perfect in weakness" (2 Corinthians 12:9).* Is it not amazing that God takes the broken parts of our lives and makes us stronger because of them? No wonder, then, that Paul continued, *"Therefore I will boast all the more gladly about my weaknesses, so that Christ's power may rest on me."*

By restating the declaration of Christ's resurrection as our highest priority, we say His mighty power is available to transform lives today and make us more than conquerors. Therefore we give our weaknesses to Him and find new power to overcome them. Thus they become available for use towards God's glory. Christian history is replete with splendid examples of this. Here are but a few:

Consider Mary Magdalene. Who but Christ can take a woman of ill repute, broken by her illegitimate life style, scorned by her own people and transform her into a fearless and godly daughter of God Almighty?

Consider Paul the apostle. Who but Christ could take a murderous self-sufficient Pharisee and break him of his pride? In Christ he became the apostle to the Gentile world and prolific writer to advance Christ's cause in every generation.

Consider John Newton, once a drunken slave trader so desperate for another drink that he sold himself into bondage. In God's grace he confronted the helplessness of his addiction to alcohol. Under Christ John Newton was transformed into a powerful preacher, pastor and hymn-writer who gave the world a hymn about his own life that is a Christian favorite because it fits every life:

Amazing grace, how sweet the sound
That saved a wretch like me;

49

I once was lost, but now I'm found;
Was blind but now I see.

Consider Charles Colson. The articulate tough guy Marine veteran lawyer who proudly wore the title "Richard Nixon's hatchet-man" was broken after a court convicted him for his part in crimes that shocked America. An encounter with God's grace in Jesus transformed him into a mighty evangelist to prisoners and apologist for the Christian faith in our generation.

Each of these is a case study in what God through the resurrected Christ is able to do in any life. The resurrection message is not only that we have life over the death that is to come, but that we have life over the death in us that used to be. Christ alone can take the very worst things in our lives and orchestrate them for good and gain. In Him people who are spiritually dead are brought to life. This same resurrected Lord of the cross called Jesus of Nazareth is still at work in our world. He is able to take that which is dead and broken about any life and breathe new life into it for the gospel's sake. What sustains the church of Jesus Christ generation after generation is not that its people are perfect but that its Lord is both perfect and resurrected.

Christ's Resurrection People

It is not only people as individuals that Christ inspires through His resurrection power. He also empowers us as groups; indeed, perhaps even more than as individuals. This is never more so than when we join together as Christ's resurrection people, the Church. I once heard my friend, one of the world's foremost missionary statesmen, John Haggai, tell the amazing story of resurrection power at work not just in one person but in a group of people who joined hands together to serve the Lord. The members of the Young Nak Church began meeting together for worship and Bible study in 1946. They were twenty-seven destitute North Korean refugees and they met in a threadbare tent on a mountain outside Seoul. One Sunday the weight of a heavy snow caused their tent to finally collapse. In that setting their young pastor suggested they build a building to establish a church that would reach out to all the people around them.

For a penniless congregation, that seemed impossible; some might even have called it an absurd idea. Then one woman in that little congregation demonstrated her commitment. She said, "I have no money but here is my wedding ring. Sell it and put whatever money you receive towards our new church building." Another said, "I own only these clothes I wear and the quilt I sleep under. Please take my quilt and sell it too. I will ask my friend if I may sleep under her quilt while she is awake." Someone else said, "I have only my spoon and rice bowl. Please take it and sell it. I will borrow my friend's spoon and rice bowl to eat." These sacrificial gifts and others like them were sold and the seemingly meager sale proceeds were invested in advancing Christ's kingdom.

As often happens when God is at work money came in from unexpected sources. It was added to funds received from the sale of those personal items. In time a new church building was constructed. Much of the work was performed by members of the congregation. Their building was no fancy cathedral but compared to an old canvas tent it looked splendid to the members of the budding congregation. Even more wonderful was the spirit they sensed God developing in their midst. It was the Spirit of their resurrected Lord and they would need it for all that lay ahead did not bid well for that young and growing group of believers.

In 1950, just as the new building was about to be dedicated, Communists from North Korea moved south. They confiscated the church building and transformed it into their ammunition depot. They declared that anyone who came near would be shot. People from that congregation wept as they prayed for God's guidance from a distance.

After United Nations forces pushed the Communists back behind the 38th Parallel, a godly elder was permitted by United Nations soldiers to enter the now much abused building and assess its condition. No one knew that some Communist soldiers were still hiding inside. When that elder entered the building the Communists set upon him from behind. They put a gun to his head. He asked for permission to pray. It was granted. He kneeled. They shot him. Realizing their presence was revealed by the gunshot the Communist soldiers ran away. Now his tombstone marks the spot where that church family found their beloved elder's body. It was the very place where he kneeled to pray.

Financial hardship, sacrifice, opposition, martyrdom, all these have been faced by the Young Nak congregation. Christ's resurrection power has sustained and inspired them in the face of all these things. Today Young Nak Church is the largest Presbyterian congregation in the world!

His Resurrection Power And Ours
"Before long, the world will not see me anymore, but you will see me. Because I live, you also will live" (John 14:19). Resurrection power! It is often simply the power to hang in when the going gets tough. In the tradition of Young Nak Church and in the tradition of the first disciples we the First Presbyterian Church of Pittsburgh ask God's help to demonstrate it to our world.

We believe in the resurrected Jesus and we invite all whose past is marked by evidence of deadness to surrender that past to Him, to watch Him transform it into something new, beautiful and powerful and to come and join us in our fellowship of service in His name.

Chapter

6

Our Highest Priority:
To Demonstrate Christ's...Love

Since we have been justified through faith, we have peace with God through our Lord Jesus Christ, through whom we have gained access by faith into this grace in which we now stand. And we rejoice in the hope of the glory of God. Not only so, but we also rejoice in our sufferings, because we know that suffering produces perseverance; perseverance, character; and character, hope. And hope does not disappoint us, because God has poured out his love into our hearts by the Holy Spirit, whom he has given us. You see, at just the right time, when we were still powerless, Christ died for the ungodly. Very rarely will anyone die for a righteous man, though for a good man someone might possibly dare to die. But God demonstrates his own love for us in this: While we were still sinners, Christ died for us.

--Romans 5:1-8

This is a true story: When Warden Lewis Lawes came to Sing Sing in 1920, he inherited the most despicable place on this continent. Warden Lawes immediately introduced reforms that treated the prisoners like people instead of things. The inmates noticed the difference right away. When they expressed gratitude, Lawes directed the credit to his wife, Kathryn. Kathryn Lawes was a disciple of Jesus and believed Christ's redemption could transform any life.

Sometimes Kathryn took her three children to visit inmates who had no visitors. They were rapists, murderers, and some of the most notorious gangsters in American history. In spite of that, she never showed fear. She encouraged prisoners known to be undergoing a particular difficulty by extending a personal touch in some thoughtful way.

In 1937, seventeen years after the Lawes arrived at Sing Sing, a car accident took Kathryn Lawes' life. The next day her casket lay in the Warden's house a quarter mile from the prison compound. At exercise time the Deputy Warden noticed the prisoners were not gathering in groups or playing basketball, as they usually did. Instead, they gathered silently around the fence that faced the home. Some of the men looked as though they were praying. He knew what they were thinking.

Leaving his station, the Deputy Warden stepped before the prisoners and said, "Men, I'm going to trust you. You can go to the house." He ordered the main gate opened. The prisoners walked through respectfully. No count was taken. No roll was called. No guards were dispatched. That evening at countdown, not one prisoner was missing. Love for one who demonstrated love for them made murderers, rapists, con artists and gangsters people to be trusted.

Such is the amazing hope God has for us in the gospel: *"God demonstrates his own love for us in this: While we were still sinners, Christ died for us."* Paul's declaration brings us face to face with Calvary's cross as the masterwork of God's redeeming love.

Having considered the proclamation priority of our Mission Statement in chapters four and five we come now to its practice priority:

We, the First Presbyterian Church of Pittsburgh, stand steadfastly for:

> *Our Foundation......the Bible, God's Word;*
> *Our Lord......Jesus Christ, God's only Son;*
> *Our highest priority......to proclaim Christ's cross*
> *and resurrection*
> **and demonstrate His love**

As Deep As It Gets

Scholarly research confirms that the apostle John, who gave us the Gospel that bears his name, lived to a ripe old age. He was in all likelihood the last of the apostles to die. In the course of his long life he made many missionary journeys to beginning churches. We can easily imagine how excited the people of those fledgling congregations must have been to welcome him. This was more than an ordinary visiting preacher or theologian. This was *"The disciple whom Jesus loved" (John 13:23)*, the final first hand witness to the resurrection and perhaps Christ's best friend. John was chosen to accompany the Lord to the meeting with Moses and Elijah on the Mount of Transfiguration and when the Lord went into Gethsemane to pray on the final evening before His trial and crucifixion. He saw it all with his own eyes.

One tradition tells of Christians eagerly gathering around the wise old John to listen to his teaching. His lesson was always the same. It was brief and to the point: *"Little children, love one another."* Having said those few words John would sit down. Sometimes the new Christians were confused. Some were a little miffed. They had, after all, looked forward enthusiastically to John's visit. Was

55

this all they would hear from the great theologian and writer who was selected to write the gospel of God's love for the world?

Finally, one day a relatively young and erudite disciple felt emboldened to speak: "Dear brother," he began, "we already knew this having read and heard it many times before. Might you not be able to give us something just a little deeper?" "My dear children," John replied, "our dear Lord's command is that we love one another. It simply does not get any deeper."

There is no confirmed record of this conversation. It is purely and simply one of the traditions of the church. Is it a myth or the truth? We have no way of knowing. This we do know: John's focus on the heart of Christ's teaching is as valid now as it ever was. The Lord's command to love is at the same time the easiest and the hardest lesson we will ever learn as Christians.

Therefore, proclamation by itself is not enough, even when it is the proclamation of the greatest news the world will ever hear; the wonder of Christ's cross and resurrection. The world we live in demands more than mere words and so it should. Therefore, we also prioritize the practice of Christ's love as an ongoing part of our ministry together.

Where is Christ's Love?
There are some things that cause reasonable people to question Christ's love. Where, for example, is a loving Christ when little children starve in Biafra?

Where was Christ when Flight 427 barreled into the hillside near Pittsburgh airport? Or, when TWA flight 800 broke apart and fell into Long Island Sound?

How was God's love demonstrated when an Amish baby died at Children's Hospital a couple of months ago?

Or, when a fifteen year old was blinded by a gunshot fired by another fifteen year old in Homewood?

Or, when a campus minister with a wife and young children was murdered while he was coming home from a Bible Study at Carnegie-Mellon University?

Where was God when a six year old beauty queen was molested and strangled in her own home at Christmas?

Rational people ask such questions and who would blame them?

Daily reports in hometown newspapers and on television in every major American city seem to speak against this truth we all want to trust, yet the death of God's Son on Calvary's cross overshadows them all. *"God demonstrates his own love for us in this: While we were still sinners, Christ died for us."* In this Scripture declaration we find the nearest thing to an answer available for now.

These words do not imply that because of Christ's death our tears are dried away instantly; or that problems disappear into thin air because we believe what Paul writes here. God's love for us does not make us immune to suffering.

The truth is that non-Christians and Christians alike question these events for they impact the lives of all of us. In many of the instances just cited Christians were the victims of suffering and loss. There is no difference between us at this point. What hurts unbelievers hurts believers also. The darkness of loss still blinds us. Nevertheless, we are satisfied to know our questions will find their answers in the morning of eternal brightness that Christ

57

procured for us on His cross. There are circumstances and situations for which none of us has perfect answers, and anyone who tells you he does is not playing straight with you.

What we do have is confidence. Jesus said He would never forsake us and we take Him at His word. That does not mean we escape loss or suffering; it means that God Himself will never leave us no matter what we face. As Christians, we believe the answer is on its way. The day will come when we will understand all these things. In the meantime, *"We see but a poor reflection as in a mirror; then we shall see face to face" (1 Corinthians 13:12).* All we have to rely upon until then is the Bible's constant assurance that God does love us, and the supreme proof of that love is the death of God's Son for us.

Everyday Love
Do not miss this love's everyday nature. It is not a past tense love of which Paul speaks. He does not write that love was demonstrated. It is being demonstrated now. There is a perpetual present tense to it. God *"demonstrates,"* says the apostle.

Some Bible statements are historical. They happened once, achieved their purpose, and were put away, as it were. *"The LORD shut (Noah) in (the ark)" (Genesis 6:16).* That happened one time a long time ago. A lot has happened in the meantime. Yet one fact about God stands unmoved every day. At the core of all things, unshaken and unshakable, is Calvary love.

This love God demonstrates for us is more than a Good Friday afternoon romance. It is the most alive love story ever. In each generation, it transforms people who do bad things into children of God. It gives those with no respect, self-respect, and those with no life, life eternal. It says that no matter what others think about us, Christ favors us before Himself. To those the world deems worthless it says He values you in terms all the wealth in the universe cannot equal. God loves you today, and that is a fact.

It is this present tense nature that calls us to demonstrate Christ's love. It is not enough to merely tell people God loves them in Jesus or that one day they will see just how much God loves them. We are called to show them God's love in Christ here and now every day. That is why we make this our ministry priority.

The Nature Of God's Love
There are many kinds of love. One builds up, exalts, and seeks the best for its beloved while another drags its beloved down to its own level. One love is nothing but lust disguised while another dreams the best for its beloved, and does all it can to help make that happen.

The love of God is greater by far than the best of human love. His love is a love with no limits that deems no price too great to pay. It is a love so all sufficient it leaves nothing for us to do but believe it with all our heart. Isn't that amazing! There are no conditions to the way God loves us. All we must do to know His love is trust Him for it.

Turn your focus to Calvary's cross. In your mind's eye see the scene there. Who was that between two thieves with pierced hands and feet, but God's only Son? No patriot ever loved like that. Nor did any mother, though a healthy mother love must surely be the nearest thing we can know to it. No human love can ever compare to Christ Jesus hanging in shame before a mocking mob. His love that day was, and still is, wide enough to embrace every person ever born; and long enough to go with us however far we wander. It was deep enough to stretch down into hell; and high enough to raise us to all God dreams for us.

A New England couple announced their engagement only a few weeks before America got involved in the Second World War. Wedding plans were postponed by the country's call. At the station as he boarded the train that would take him towards basic training, they pledged to write daily letters to each other, which they did. As each letter arrived she read it and dreamed of the day he would come back from the war.

Then, without warning, his letters stopped coming. "I'll get one tomorrow," she thought at first. Still, weeks went by and no letters came. She took the letters he had written from the drawer, where she treasured each one, and untied the ribbon that held them together. She read and re-read each sentence. It was not the same as getting a new letter every day, but it was something to hold to in hope that a letter might come soon.

Finally, one day a letter came. His name and number were on the envelope but the writing was different. She ripped the envelope apart and found one sheet inside. One sheet! One sheet that ripped away her dreams.

He wrote, "Something has happened and I have terrible news for you. I was severely wounded in battle and have lost both my arms. Someone else writes this for me. I love you as much as ever, but feel I must release you from the obligation of our engagement. Move on with your life. You will be better off without me."

Tears rolled off her cheeks and blotched the ink as she read his letter again. She took pen and paper in hand, but could find no words to answer. It was too hard. She decided not to write back. Instead, at the station where once they kissed goodbye, she boarded a train for New York. Once there, she purchased a ticket on a ship headed for Europe. In a strange land she found her way to the military hospital listed on that envelope. Tearfully, she searched among the wounded and dying for the man who had given her his ring. When she found him, she threw her arms around his neck, kissed him, and said, "From this day forward, my arms are your arms, just as my heart is yours. I will take care of you always. There is nothing that we cannot do together."

Love In Theory Versus Love In Reality
In Berkeley, California, I was told about a scholarly confirmed bachelor who wrote a treatise on the theme, "What Is Love?" His research was extensive, lasting several months. It involved hours of interviews, listening to lectures and reading books in the library. After gathering his material he prepared his work for presentation. He called a stenography service and asked that someone come to his study to type his manuscript. Soon after that a young woman arrived to do that work. As they encountered one another for the first time something unexpected and unusual happened. Their eyes met. Each of them felt a strange feeling sweep through them. Their pulses quickened. It was love at first sight. Suddenly the subject of that bachelor's paper was more than just an academic project to him. In one exciting meeting he learned more about love than all the research in the world could ever teach him.

So it is with God's love. It must be more than theory to us. We must relax ourselves in His presence and let Him love us. When we do His love becomes our own and we know that although *"God so loved the world that he gave his one and only Son, that whoever believes in him shall not perish but have eternal life" (John 3:16)*, He would love us all alone if we were the only person in the world. Having experienced that love personally it becomes our duty; no, more than that, it becomes our delight to pass it on to others in Christ's name.

Thus we demonstrate His love for we know that Christ has no arms but our arms with which to embrace those who feel unloved. He has no heart but our heart to love the lost, the lonely, the broken and the wounded people in our generation. If there is one thing more wonderful than to know personally this love of God we receive every day in Jesus it must surely be that He invites us to pass it on for Him.

At First Presbyterian Church of Pittsburgh our Mission Statement says, *"Our highest priority is to proclaim Christ's cross and resurrection and demonstrate His love"* because we believe these faith principles of proclamation and practice are inseparably linked. Words without action are a sign of arrogance. In the apostle Paul's words they makes us no more than, *"clanging cymbals" (1 Corinthians 13:1).*

Our Mission Statement announces our intention to make this declaration more than a noble high sounding sentence by putting shoe leather on it. This is a worthy goal for all who follow Jesus. As we link arms and hearts with other Christians there is nothing we cannot do together for Him who loved us all the way to Calvary's cross and loves us still.

Chapter

7

Our Highest Goal:
That All May Know
The Saving Power of the Gospel

"For God so loved the world that he gave his one and only Son, that whoever believes in him shall not perish but have eternal life. For God did not send his Son into the world to condemn the world, but to save the world through him. Whoever believes in him is not condemned, but whoever does not believe stands condemned already because he has not believed in the name of God's one and only Son...Whoever believes in the Son has eternal life, but whoever rejects the Son will not see life, for God's wrath remains on him."

--John 3:16-18,36

An ancient tale pictures billions of people scattered on a great plane before God's judgment throne at the end of the world. This is the ultimate final examination. Some huddled and prayed fervently for mercy. Some colluded to make excuses for their misdeeds. Others talked belligerently. The heightened volume of their uneasy voices was easily heard above the others: "How can God judge us?" one agitated voice asked, "What does He understand about what we have suffered?"

Suddenly a woman from the latter group rolled up her shirtsleeve and revealed her Auschwitz tattoo. At the same time she lifted her voice angrily: "What could God who sits in heaven know about the beatings, torture and death our people endured in the prison camps?" An African-American man's open shirt collar exposed an ugly rope burn. He unbuttoned another button to make it easier for others to see. "We suffocated in slave ships and toiled in hot sun until death was our best hope for freedom," he cried out. "We were lynched for being black. What could God know about the evils of racism?" Another man declared, "I'll tell you, God could never understand how lucky He had it to live a sheltered life with no tears, fear, hunger nor hatred."

From the membership of this group a coalition was appointed to seek common ground. One was chosen to represent each concern present that day. The final composition of the association they formed included a Jew, an African-American, an Indian Untouchable, an illegitimate person and a homeless person. Together they planned their defense and prepared to present their case succinctly.

Before God could be their judge, they said, let Him experience something of their suffering on earth. He must be willing to live on earth as a man. Let Him be a Jew of the under classes, born under such circumstance that people would question His legitimacy. Charge Him to champion some unpopular, but just, cause and experience the hate filled response of a status quo determined to destroy him. In the face of that, He must work for peace. Towards the end, let Him experience betrayal by a trusted close friend and be indicted on false charges. Drag Him before a prejudiced jury and cowardly judge who will turn Him over to be punished even though He did nothing wrong. Throw Him in prison where He will endure beatings at the hands of cowards who will care not at all that He is unarmed and unable to defend Himself. Take Him, at last, to the public square to endure complete abandonment, public humiliation and the most ignoble death society can imagine.

Their list completed the belligerent mob's leaders read it aloud before their followers. As they read it, deadly silence fell over them all. Apart from the reader, no one said a word. No one protested. No one scorned. No one moved. Instead, they hung their heads in shame for they realized that God in Jesus Christ had already served their sentence. They could catalog no punishment nor injustice which He had not already suffered.

"God did not send his Son into the world to condemn the world, but to save the world through him."

Our Highest Goal
We, the First Presbyterian Church of Pittsburgh, stand steadfastly for:

Our Foundation......the Bible, God's Word;
Our Lord......Jesus Christ, God's only Son;
Our highest priority......to proclaim Christ's cross and resurrection ;
Our Highest Goal......that all may know the saving power of the Gospel...

Everything we have said so far is directed towards an objective or focused on a goal. That goal has two parts to it. Those parts form the subject of this chapter and the one that follows. The first part of our goal is, *"That all may know the saving power of the Gospel."*

The Saving Power Of The Gospel
If we focus on this tenet alone, we will be in an increasingly rare company even among the churches. If today's church in our nation and in many parts of the world is deficient in one area more than

any other, it is that this most central Scriptural command of passing on our faith by word and deed is largely disregarded. We have lost the sense of urgency that once caused us to focus on evangelism and missions as every Christian's central focus. Every major mainline denomination is suffering a membership loss as a result. It is sad but true that the vast majority of Christians die having never offered themselves to lead another person to saving faith in Christ. At First Presbyterian Church of Pittsburgh we aspire to break this self-defeating trend.

What is *the saving power of the gospel?* The Bible speaks of it under three powerful concepts: Justification, Sanctification, Glorification.

The Past Tense: We Were Saved

In the past, we were saved. God *"chose us in Christ before the creation of the world"* Paul tells the church at Ephesus through his epistle *(Ephesians 1:4)*. He writes in the past tense that God *"chose us"* to establish an already accomplished action.

Through this already accomplished action on God's part we were justified. To be justified is to be declared "just-as-if-I'd" never sinned. The key word in this context is, "declared." It is not that we are sinless but that God has proclaimed us so. Neither does it mean that we no longer sin but, rather, that we *"Rejoice in God through our Lord Jesus Christ, through whom we have now received reconciliation" (Romans 5:11)*. Notice again the past tense nature of the sentence passing this gospel truth to us. Thus it allows us to know that our reconciliation to God is an already accomplished fact.

There was a day when despite our sin God treated us as though we were sinless. He certified us to be innocent. Some Christians remember the very moment they heard this good news for the first time. They can tell the exact time, date and place they realized they were forgiven. Others may not have that recollection because they were raised in the faith and put their trust in Christ for forgiveness before their memory processes fully comprehended what happened. Whatever the case, each of us surely remembers when we realized that God graciously included us in Christ's atoning death.

Jackie grew up in the church. As a child of the covenant she received baptism in infancy. She learned later that it happened during her first trip out after she was released from the newborn unit at the hospital. Before the congregation of God's people her parents presented her and pledged to raise her in the nurture and admonition of the Lord, to teach her the great verities of the Christian faith and to pray with and for her. They kept their promise with great faithfulness. From her earliest days Jackie was aware of Christ's love for her. She does not remember exactly when she prayed asking Jesus to come into her heart. What she does remember, however, is that when she was in college she gradually came to an understanding of precisely what that meant in terms of her eternal soul and God's claim on her life. She says, "After months of trying to figure it out it finally all came together for me. My heart leaped inside me and I knew that God had called me His own and nothing could ever separate me from His love." She knew in that instant that she must spend her life in service to Christ. Today she nurses sick children at a mission hospital in East Africa.

The line from a great old gospel hymn fits her story perfectly:
He loved me e'er I knew Him and all my love is due Him.

Jackie found the victory that Christ alone provided when He saved her on Calvary's cross. She came with the faith of a child and God grew that faith within her heart until the moment she realized that Christ had been in her life before she even knew it.

Others tell a different story. Francis of Assisi was born into a wealthy central Italian family in 1182. Because of his inherited wealth and loose spirit Francis saw little need for an education. Preferring parties to school, he received only a few years of formal education and spent his early life as a playboy. Duty to country called and Francis enlisted in the army. His position in society guaranteed him an immediate commission to officer status but it did not guarantee his safety in battle. Captured by the enemy, he spent a year as a prisoner of war. Whilst in prison he fell ill and feared he might die. In that context he surrendered his life to Christ.

It was an amazing conversion experience. Francis, who had little use for education before, now read every book he could find. Learning about the encounter between Jesus and the rich young ruler through reading the Bible, Francis promised God that if his life was spared he would give everything he had to help the poor.

Long before San Francisco, a city named in his honor, opened its Golden Gate Saint Francis opened the gate to his gold. True to his word, upon his release from prison, Francis sold all his possessions including his shoes. He spent the money he made from the sale of his earthly possessions caring for others. He was left with only the set of clothes he was wearing. His parents were convinced their son was mentally ill. Francis' father, Pietro, concerned that his son would give away the entire family fortune, disinherited him. Even that could not cool Francis' commitment to serving Christ. He supported himself by repairing chapels around Assisi. People who knew the playboy Francis before his conversion observed the difference Christ brought about in his life. Many of his former playboy friends were so impressed by his new found concern for the sick and needy that they followed Francis' example and sacrificed their own wealth for the gospel. Thus began the Order of the Begging Brothers.

This band of former party-boys went out two by two spreading Christ's message of new life and service. They took their message throughout Italy, France, Germany, Hungary, Spain and England. Wherever they went the gospel was preached and hospitals and schools were established in Christ's name.

Later Francis formed an order for his former female playmates who also sought to make a difference in Christ's name. This order known as the Order of the Poor Clares was named after a wealthy young socialite called Clare who also sold everything to follow Jesus.

Two years after Francis died in 1226, Pope Gregory IX canonized him as an official saint of the church. Soon after, the Order of the Begging Brothers became the Order of St. Francis or the Franciscans. Twenty years after Francis' death his order had constructed over nine thousand homes, hospitals and schools.

For Jackie the knowledge of being saved came gradually. For Francis of Assisi it came suddenly. Yet the results were the same; a life was transformed and dedicated to serving the King of Kings. Such is the difference Christ makes in the saving power of the gospel. *"For it is by grace you have been saved, through faith—and this not from yourselves, it is the gift of God-- not by works, so that no one can boast. For we are God's workmanship, created in Christ Jesus to do good works, which God prepared in advance for us to do"* *(Ephesians 2:8-10).*

No one can seriously consider what it means to be saved by God through Christ's sacrifice and remain disinterested, unconcerned and uninvolved in making Christ's message known.

The Present Tense: We Are Being Saved

Paul addresses his message *"To us who are being saved"* (1 *Corinthians 1:18)*. His Greek words in the imperfect tense signify an action that, although incomplete, is under way. There is a sense in which God's "Work in Progress" sign hangs on each of our lives. Sanctification is under way as the work of God's free grace. Once, we were saved from sin's penalty. Now we are being saved from sin's power. We are not yet perfect for, in Francis Shaeffer's words, "If you'll only settle for perfection or nothing, you'll always end up with nothing." *"Sin shall not be your master, because you are not under law, but under grace" (Romans 6:14)*.

Perhaps no part of Scripture makes this more plain than Paul's confession to the Romans: *"What I do is not the good I want to do; no, the evil I do not want to do—this I keep on doing" (Romans 7:19)*. These words frame the story of Paul's personal struggle after his conversion to Christ. If you are real, they tell your story too. All who belong to Christ live between two worlds. One is the world that now is. The other is the world of what we aspire to make for Him who loved us all the way to Calvary and loves us still.

The Future Tense: We Shall Be Saved

"Since we have now been justified by his blood, how much more shall we be saved from God's wrath through him!" (Romans 5:9). We were saved from sin's penalty. That is salvation's past tense. We are being saved from its power. This is its present tense. One day, we shall be saved even from sin's presence. Christ has prepared a sinless environment in eternity for us. Such is God's promise concerning our salvation's future tense. The salvation that began in eternity past and was consummated on Calvary's cross, continues to work in us through our sanctification. It will be completed in our glorification.

Justification! Sanctification! Glorification! The three tenses of salvation. In Paul's words, *"Those He predestined, He also called; those He called, He also justified; those He justified, He also glorified" (Romans 8:30)*. In the queen of the sciences, theology, these are three key components of what we call the, "Ordo saludas," the order of salvation.

What Are We Saved From?
Sadly, too often neither our culture nor the church squares with this issue. *"Whoever rejects the Son will not see life, for God's wrath remains on him."* We are saved from God's anger. We who are saved will not endure His final punishment. This is what gives us the imperative in our preaching, teaching and ministry.

An elderly Russian woman devoutly kissed the feet of a statue of Christ in the presence of a Soviet soldier. The soldier immediately challenged her with this question, "Babushka, will you kiss Stalin's feet?" "Of course," she replied, "as soon as he dies for me, rises again and says he still loves me!" That dear woman understood the gospel for that is what Christ did for us.

Are You Saved?
"Brother, are you saved? Sister, are you saved?" Comedians, even some who say they are Christians, make fun of those questions. The world makes caricatures of them. In spite of that we must always remember, *"Salvation is found in no one else, for there is no other name under heaven given to men by which we must be saved" (Acts 4:12)*.

Are You Saving?
Only Christ can save and He enlists us in His service with the privilege of telling His salvation plan. Most often, it seems, God uses more than one person to introduce someone to new life in

Jesus Christ. Yet, the fact remains that we are all charged with telling the lost how to be saved. We may be the first or the second person to tell someone. We may be the twentieth, or thirtieth, or fiftieth; or, we may be the last—the one who actually sees someone receive Christ by faith. What number we are is not important. What is eternally important is that we accept our assignment to be a witness for the saving power of the Gospel of Christ Jesus.

How long has it been since you last invited someone to receive the Lord or to come join you where you knew Christ's claim on every life would be presented? At First Presbyterian Church of Pittsburgh we have been made stewards of God's good news and good news is worth sharing. Therefore, *"Each one should use whatever gift he has received to serve others, faithfully administering God's grace in its various forms. If anyone speaks, he should do it as one speaking the very words of God. If anyone serves, he should do it with the strength God provides, so that in all things God may be praised through Jesus Christ. To him be the glory and the power for ever and ever. Amen" (1 Peter 4:10,11).*

Chapter

8

...A Life Worthy Of Christ's Calling

We constantly pray for you, that our God may count you worthy of his calling, and that by his power he may fulfill every good purpose of yours and every act prompted by your faith. We pray this so that the name of our Lord Jesus may be glorified in you, and you in him, according to the grace of our God and the Lord Jesus Christ.

--2 Thessalonians 1:11-12

From time to time the media brings news of some cult that misunderstands the central thrust of Christ's message and our responsibility. Usually such movements are confused by a hodgepodge theology that, because it was not corrected in a timely and constructive fashion, lost its balance. One such movement was the Heavens Gate group whose people settled near San Diego, California, and awaited the arrival of the Hale-Bob comet which they believed would deliver them from this world altogether. Another was the Jim Jones group that settled for a time in seclusion in Guyana and waited there believing the Lord would come soon for them. There are many others. Who among us has not thought at some time of "running away from it all?" The peaceful seclusion that life alone, or perhaps with a few specially chosen friends or family members, seems to offer can seem very appealing to the human imagination. The words of the old Country

and Western song, *This world is not my home, I'm just a-passin'
through*, has a place in all our hearts from time to time. Life,
perhaps particularly for serious disciples of Jesus, is not easy in
this world and escape seems not unattractive when times are tough.
Yet, Christ's call never calls us to separate from the world.
Indeed, the Lord who was *"tempted in every way, just as we are"
(Hebrews 4:15)* specifically cautions us against the potential perils
of isolationism: *"No branch can bear fruit by itself; it must remain
in the vine. Neither can you bear fruit unless you remain in me"
(John 15:4).* Because the Thessalonian Christians also were familiar
with the temptation to look for a way out of this world, Paul writes
them a letter that is intensely practical for them as well as for us.

In a sense Paul's second Thessalonian letter can be called a
corrective for its predecessor; not because First Thessalonians is
incorrect, but because parts of it were misunderstood and
misinterpreted by those Christians to whom it was initially
addressed. In the first letter Paul wrote powerfully comforting and
encouraging words about Christ's second coming. Paul's words so
captured the imagination of many Thessalonians that they believed
the day of Christ's return so imminent that many of them stopped
working their regular jobs to await His appearing. Now Paul,
having heard this, writes from Corinth some months after the first
letter to clarify this misunderstanding and to encourage the
Thessalonian Christians, and us, to focus on practical Christian
living. As he does in other places, Paul sets us a model for how to
deal with difficult issues in the church. He responds quickly with
words which, though firm, are encouraging.

Good News Travels Fast

Paul recognized the far reaching implications of anything that
happened in Thessalonica in his day. This seaport city lying at the
foothills of Mount Khortiatis, had an impact far beyond other cities
of similar size when Paul established a church there. Then, as

now, it was known as a gem of the ocean. A prosperous port and trading center, it was a recognized place for people to gather and discuss the things that were on their minds and hearts. Thessalonica was, therefore, an information center. Ships from all over the world docked there to load and unload cargo. The sailors who traveled on those ships took news from Thessalonica all over the world. Needless to say, misinformation and misunderstanding about the gospel in a place like that could have far reaching consequences. On the other hand, good news well told would also travel far making a positive mark on many lives. So, when Paul writes his second letter he does so with a sense of urgency.

He tells the Thessalonians that Jesus may indeed return at any moment. Therefore, Christians must live in a state of readiness, prepared to greet the Lord at any moment. On the other hand, Jesus may tarry. It could be a long time by human reckoning before He returns. If He delays the people of the church need to consider how to live in the meantime: *"With this in mind, we constantly pray for you, that our God may count you worthy of his calling, and that by his power he may fulfill every good purpose of yours and every act prompted by your faith."*

A Life Worthy of Christ's Calling
We, the First Presbyterian Church of Pittsburgh, stand steadfastly for:

Our Foundation......the Bible, God's Word;
Our Lord......Jesus Christ, God's only Son;
Our highest priority......to proclaim Christ's cross
and resurrection ;
Our Highest Goal......that all may know
the saving power of the Gospel
and live a life worthy of Christ's calling

75

In the World But Not Of the World
In some ways the Mission Statement phrase we are considering in this chapter might be called the tough part of our life together in Christ. It calls us to something that, at least for now, seems humanly impossible: *"Live a life worthy of Christ's calling."* The key word is *live.* As Christians we are called to live in the present world. However, we are called to not live like this world. A life worthy of our Lord's calling means we do not disconnect ourselves from life in this present world. We do, however, come apart from those things which the world does that dishonor Christ and break God's commandments. We become salt and light bringing a positive influence wherever we can in our society.

So, also this phrase might also be called our Mission Statement's practical phrase. In that sense it is the easiest one to keep for how we are to keep it is spelled out in the Mission Statement itself. In a generation that often seems to be lost in a spiritual and moral fog it clearly declares who we are. These words tell all who see them or hear them that this is who we plan to be until Christ returns. God helping us, this is where we will stand for Christ and for Christ alone. We will be people whose only foundation is the Bible which we receive as God's word. Our Lord shall be Jesus Christ, God's only Son, and no other. Our first priority is to proclaim Christ's cross and resurrection. Our supreme goal is that people everywhere may know the saving power of the Gospel of Jesus Christ who alone is worthy to save and that they may live a life worthy of His calling.

Grace At Work
Paul opens his letter by commending the Christians of Thessalonica for their growing faith: *"Your faith is growing more and more" (2 Thessalonians 1:3).* As the founding pastor of the church in Thessalonica, nothing brings Paul more joy than news of faith growth there.

Every pastor feels a sense of great delight and fulfillment when this happens. As I look over our congregation when we are together, I am reminded and grateful for the penetrating positive difference God has brought about, and is bringing about, in the lives of some people. For more than two centuries God has been doing a mighty work both in and through our First Presbyterian Church of Pittsburgh family for which I praise Him every day. Not long ago, I taught a Bible Study to our young adult group. Their attentive listening, astute questions and absorbing spirits brought me great delight. Memories of that evening have caused my soul to soar each time I have thought about it. May God be praised for what He is doing there and in other places among us! That is one of the reasons why our church encourages our people to be steady students of the Scriptures both alone and in groups such as that.

Practical Love
Paul's commendation to the Thessalonian Christians continues with another word of gratitude: *"The love everyone of you has for each other is increasing"* *(2 Thessalonians 1:3)*. Wherever the true church of Christ meets love is always in the air. *"By this all men will know that you are my disciples, if you love one another"* *(John 13:35)*. Eleven times the New Testament calls for this demonstration of love between the people of God as a required part of what it means to be one of the Lord's disciples.

Now, the love Christ decrees among us is not some sloppy emotion than runs high and low according to our mood of the moment. It is perhaps best demonstrated by a constant spirit of caring for others within Christ's body, the church. At First Presbyterian Church of Pittsburgh we work hard to foster a pure sense of caring for our people. There is genuine concern among us when we learn about someone's need of friendship, fellowship, support or other life necessity. We place a high priority on meeting such needs in the Lord's name. We do this not only for our own people but for others as we become aware of needs we might meet together for Christ's glory. As the pastor of this congregation, I hear stories almost every day of people in our church family embracing each other with wonderfully practical love, and extending Christ's love to others not of our fellowship. Paul saw this same spirit at work in Thessalonica and commended the Christians there for this evidence of a life worthy of Christ's calling.

Perseverance Under Pressure

Another evidence of Christ's work for which Paul commends these Christians is their spirit of stick-to-it-iveness: *"We boast about your perseverance and faith in all the persecutions and trials you are enduring."* For *perseverance* Paul chooses *hupome*, a strong Greek word meaning more than mere idle endurance. This word *hupome* means these Christians understand suffering in the context of blessings and respond to it in constructive ways.

True suffering is a gift from God: *"It has been granted to you on behalf of Christ not only to believe on him, but also to suffer for him" (Philippians 1:29).* Suffering understood in that light provides an opportunity for us to steadfastly demonstrate our Christian mettle. There is something in our nature that does not readily consider suffering a privilege. Yet, there is nothing that demonstrates Christ's presence in us quite like the way we face suffering. Adversity tells more about our commitment to the Lord of the cross than all the Bibles we can carry under our arms. It is said that the blood of the martyrs is the seed of the church. Christian history certainly demonstrates this. In every century there are testimonies about Christians thriving out of suffering. How we face tough times is the evidence of a *"life worthy of his calling"* being lived out in us.

The Righteous Judgment of God

Contrary to what some people may think, preachers do not enjoy talking about fire and brimstone. Jeremiah wept at the thought of it. Jesus did too as He peered over Jerusalem. Emotionally healthy people get no joy thinking about the judgment of others. Having said that, however, any preacher who fails to deal with the subject when Scripture raises it is being unfaithful to Christ's call. Paul tells the Thessalonians that there is a present judgment and a future judgment. *"All this is evidence that God's judgment is right."* He chooses present tense words indicating that this judgment is here and now.

We have already seen that our response to God, (*"growing faith"*); to one another, (*"increasing love"*); and to adversity (*"positive perseverance"*) tells the world that Christ is doing His work in us to make us worthy of His calling. This, says the apostle, also indicates that God is making good decisions concerning us.

In addition to this present time judgment, Paul writes that God also has a future judgment in mind. His words move to the future tense: *"God is just: He will pay back trouble to those who trouble you"* (2 Thessalonians 1:6). We see cruelty and unfairness all across the universe. Where is fairness? Where is equity? Good people ask these questions. The Bible message is clear: God's arm is not short. His judgment may not always be swift by our standards, but it is always sure. Those who make trouble for His children will reap a bitter harvest and that without exception.

Intercessory Prayer

Paul, having said that Christ's revelation of Himself among the Thessalonians will bring judgment on the unsaved, rest for the saved, and glory for the Lord through His people, offers a prayer of intercession for these Christians. It is this prayer that forms the backdrop for this phrase in our Mission Statement. Paul prays that they may carry on to fruition every resolution for good among them and every work that demonstrates faith. In short, their walk is to be a demonstration of their talk. His hope for them, and surely for us also, is that Christ who will be glorified in His return will also be glorified now in the lives of all who love Him.

This word is a call to practical Christian living in each church and in every generation of Christians and we receive it as that at First Presbyterian Church of Pittsburgh. Therefore, we plan our lives now in subservience to the Lord. *"A life worthy"* means living between now and the time Christ comes, whether sooner or later, in obedience to Him. My friend, R.C. Sproul writes a magazine column called, *Right Now Counts Forever!* He is right. It does. What we do in the present matters. God reckons it eternally important. Our behavior has lasting consequences.

"That our God may count you worthy..." A life worthy of God is not earned. Like the saving grace of the gospel it is a free gift. Nobody is capable of getting God's approval through human goodness and efforts. The way we receive God's approval is through appreciating His love and responding to it in practical everyday ways. That is why Paul does not tell these Christians to live a life worthy. He says he prays they will live such a life. We can live such a life only in God's power.

"We make it our goal to please him," (2 Corinthians 5:9). In the best selling Christian novel of all time, *In His Steps*, Charles M. Sheldon speaks of the practical living out of the gospel for every Christian disciple. He suggests that we approach each decision and every situation in the context of a simple, yet profoundly spiritual question: "What would Jesus do?"

His Life In Us

What would Jesus do if He was in your place or mine? This question always has validity because Jesus is in our place: *"I have been crucified with Christ and I no longer live, but Christ lives in me. The life I live in the body, I live by faith in the Son of God, who loved me and gave himself for me" (Galatians 2:20).* If it is true that *"Christ lives in me,"* then asking how He would act or respond in each circumstance I face is a very practical outworking of His life in me. Through consistent Bible study and prayer God directs us to this question's answers for all of life. In finding the answer and putting it into action we will become the mind, heart, arms, legs, feet, and hands of Jesus in our city and in our world.

Why should we want to do this? Because we love Him and there is a reason for that love: *"We love because he first loved us" (1 John 4:19).* If there are little children in your life you understand this. We love them not because they always behave perfectly but because of who they are. Most of us hope that when they realize they are in no fear of losing our love they will want to behave in ways that are good, just and honorable. The same is true in a spiritual sense. When we realize God's love is an act of free grace, it is not earned, nor is it motivated by our obedience we want to do everything we can to please Him.

God *so* loved us that He gave up His Son for us. The Story of "Baby M" a few years ago illustrated this point from a different perspective. A surrogate mother offered to bear a child for a childless couple. All went well until she saw the child soon after it was born. Suddenly a bond developed that we all knew existed but that no one seemed to have planned for in this case. The childless couple argued that since they initiated the plans and paid all the fees the baby belonged to them. The mother, however, spoke simply of her love for her child. There is no greater force nor higher motivation for people than love and popular opinion turned in her favor.

What could I ever do that would motivate you to willingly give up a child for me? Nothing! What would compel you to choose to sacrifice a child for anyone? Nothing, but totally indescribable love. Such is God's love for us: *"God so loved the world that he gave his one and only Son, that whoever believes in him shall not perish but have eternal life" (John 3:16).*

What will we do in response to that? We will try every way we can to live a life worthy of His calling.

It Takes Time
A great story tells of an aged man, an accomplished artist, who was applying the finishing touches to a bronze sculpture. Day after day he kept on filing, scraping and polishing every surface of his masterpiece. "When will it be done?" an observer asked him. "Never," the grand old artist replied. "I just keep on improving it until they come to take it away."

The same can be said of us. Because our salvation is complete in Christ heaven is our guarantee. Yet, when it comes to being perfect we all have a long way to go. The good news is that God keeps working on us day after day. One day He will come and take us away. After that we will be with Him forever. Until then, we try to remember to demonstrate trust in Him. An acorn is not made into an oak tree in a day. It takes time. A great scholar was not made wise by one day of schooling. It takes time. One touch of an artist's brush never made a painting a masterpiece. It takes time. Planting seeds happens in a day. Reaping a harvest takes time. Becoming what we are designed to be in Christ does not happen instantly. It takes time. Be encouraged, child of God. Your time will come.

The Relentless Pursuit of Excellence For Christ
"With this in mind, we constantly pray for you, that our God may count you worthy of his calling, and that by his power he may fulfill every good purpose of yours and every act prompted by your faith."
What a beautiful portrait of the Christian life these words lay before us. Goodness brings its own pleasure. There is a depth of satisfaction that comes from doing God's will well that no words can describe and no tongue can tell. Loving acts, gracious words, thoughtful deeds, generous affirmations all work to bring God pleasure. And the result? The mutual glorification of Christ in us in this present time and our final glorification with Him in our Father's house forever and ever.

Chapter

9

Our Strength: The Holy Spirit

May the grace of the Lord Jesus Christ, and the love of God, and the fellowship of the Holy Spirit be with you all.

--2 Corinthians 13:14

Having considered each of the others in turn we now look at the final great tenet of conviction in our Mission Statement:

We, the First Presbyterian Church of Pittsburgh, stand steadfastly for:

Our Foundation......the Bible, God's Word;
Our Lord......Jesus Christ, God's only Son;
Our highest priority......to proclaim Christ's cross
and resurrection ;
Our Highest Goal......that all may know
the saving power of the Gospel
and live a life worthy of Christ's calling;
Our Strength......The Holy Spirit.

It has already been clearly stated that each pillar on which we stand calls us to a challenge too strenuous for any of us to achieve in our own strength. So, we look for a strength beyond ourselves. That strength comes from the Holy Spirit. He is the subject of this final chapter.

Having died on the cross and risen again, Jesus ascended into heaven forty days later. There was nothing left for us to do to be saved and assured of heaven except to trust Him.

Yet, God's work in the world was not completed, nor is it yet. Christ established His Church and promised it a supernatural power unlike anything the world had seen before: *"You will receive power when the Holy Spirit comes on you; and you will be my witnesses in Jerusalem, and in all Judea and Samaria, and to the ends of the earth" (Acts 1:8).*

This promise came fully alive ten days after Christ's ascension into heaven and fifty days after He rose from the grave. Jesus sent His Holy Spirit into His Church. This empowerment of His people by the Holy Spirit signaled that Jesus' work was now complete. He came from heaven. Now, having conquered death, He has returned to heaven. Before returning He entrusted us with a message of certain salvation to declare to an uncertain world. The Holy Spirit is God's empowering Agent to bring that message to life in us individually and collectively.

No member of the Holy Trinity has suffered more at the hands of those who practice theological quackery than the Holy Spirit. From the old fashioned snake oil salesman of a century or more ago to today's practitioners of health and wealth theology the Spirit has been maligned, misrepresented and misinterpreted. This is unfortunate, yet this is the world in which we live and minister together for Christ's sake.

The God Who Has It All Together
"Hear, O Israel: The LORD our God, the LORD is one" *(Deuteronomy 6:4)*. These words called the Shema in Israel form the crux of historic Jewish theology. They declared to the polytheistic nations all around them that Israel was monotheistic. The other nations could choose to have numerous different gods if they wanted but Israel would have no one but the Lord God.

"Jehovah our LORD is One," the Shema prophet shouted. An equally acceptable translation would be, *"Jehovah our LORD is together."* The Hebrew word *echad,* translated, *one,* frequently means a single unit composed of inseparable parts. For example, in Genesis 2:4 it speaks of the man being *one* with his wife. They are separate personalities yet God regards them as united. Similarly, in Numbers 12:32 *echad* describes the cluster of grapes the spies brought back from Canaan. Although each grape is separate, all finally are joined together at the stem as though they were one. In short, to their neighboring nations, the Israelites through the Shema, were saying that Israel needed only one God who would meet every need and they found Him in Jehovah.

The Eternal Love Triangle
"May the grace of the Lord Jesus Christ, and the love of God, and the fellowship of the Holy Spirit be with you all." These are often the concluding words with which we close our worship services. In many ways they are the most important words we can hear because without the Holy Spirit's fellowship the Gospel message is powerless for us. Without Him we cannot grow in the knowledge and love of God. Without Him we have no energy to evangelize the lost. Without Him our desire to worship God with our lips and our lifestyle is weak at best.

When Paul the apostle signed off with this benediction in his letter to the Corinthians he probably had no idea that it would be among the most memorable sentences he would ever pen.   In addition to being a beautiful benediction, they also provide us with a wonderfully solid theological statement about the unity of the Godhead. They do so by speaking at the same time about God the Son, God the Father and God the Holy Spirit. Moreover, they assign the role each One plays in our lives every day.

"The grace of our Lord Jesus Christ," reminds us that Christ's grace is always freely available. We need that for we all sin and find ourselves in need of Christ's forgiveness. *"The love of God"* says that we are always loved by our Father in heaven. Finally, *"The fellowship of the Holy Spirit,"* tells us that we have a powerful Friend and Companion traveling with us wherever we go.   All of these are a sign of God's tripartite eternal loving nature as Father, Son and Holy Spirit.

David's penetrating question brings both comfort and conviction to us: *"Where can I go from your Spirit? Where can I flee from your presence? If I go up to the heavens, you are there; if I make my bed in the depths, you are there. If I rise on the wings of the dawn, if I settle on the far side of the sea, even there your hand will guide me, your right hand will hold me fast. If I say, 'Surely the darkness will hide me and the light become night around me,' even the darkness will not be dark to you; the night will shine like the day, for darkness is as light to you" (Psalm 139:7-12).* We are loved everywhere for all eternity.

Growing up in Ireland, I learned that back in 1871 Philipp Bliss wrote a hymn which brings the same sense of comfort to children in every generation:

God is always near me,
Hearing what I say,
Knowing all my thoughts and deeds,
All my work and play.

God is always near me;
In the darkest night
He can see me just the same
As by mid-day light.

God is always near me,
Though so young and small;
Not a look or word or thought,
But God knows them all.

What more could any of us want than this? We are loved with grace from Jesus. We are loved with a never ceasing love from the Father. Finally, we are loved with ever near companionship from the Holy Spirit.

Who Is The Holy Spirit?
A member of our Tuesday Noon Boost congregation told me about a motivational speaker who spoke in our city not long ago. In the course of an otherwise helpful speech he attempted to describe God's power working in each of our lives to help us achieve success in business. He likened this "power" to the "Force" in the Star Wars movies. Later he closed his talk by quoting a benediction for another threesome, the benediction of the Star Wars trilogy, "May the Force be with you," without seeming to recognize the difference between the blessing of George Lucas and the eternal God. It is possible to think of the Holy Spirit as nothing more than that; just a force. When we do, however, the force becomes a farce and we miss what Jesus taught us about the Holy Spirit.

The Holy Spirit is a person. The Nicean Council which met in 325AD declared: *"We believe in the Holy Spirit, the Lord and giver of life, who proceedeth from the Father and the Son."* In doing so, they helped clarify the relationship of the Holy Spirit to God the Father and God the Son.

Jesus taught this too in His farewell talk with the disciples: *"I will ask the Father, and he will give you another Counselor to be with you forever-- the Spirit of truth. The world cannot accept him, because it neither sees him nor knows him. But you know him, for he lives with you and will be in you" (John 14:16,17).* Christ's choice of the personal pronouns, *him* and *he* and not "it" makes plain that He regards the Holy Spirit as a person and not merely a power or object.

The Holy Spirit also uses such personal pronouns when He refers to Himself: *"While they were worshiping the Lord and fasting, the Holy Spirit said, 'Set apart for me Barnabas and Saul for the work to which I have called them.' So after they had fasted and prayed, they placed their hands on them and sent them off" (Acts 13:2,3).* Through these and other Bible passages we safely conclude that God gives us more than a power to accompany and empower us. God gives us a Person who is inseparably connected with the Father and the Son. Thus the Holy Spirit is not only a person but a divine person.

Older Than Dirt

The rural South is a gold-mine of quaint verbal expressions. One of my favorites describes a person well along in years: "He is older than dirt."

In truth it can be said of the Holy Spirit that He truly is older than dirt, for the Scripture tells us so: *"In the beginning God created the heavens and the earth. Now the earth was formless and empty, darkness was over the surface of the deep, and the Spirit of God was hovering over the water" (Genesis 1:1,2).* Here we see that the Holy Spirit was present at creation before the earth was formed. The record then adds, *"God said, 'Let the water under the sky be gathered to one place, and let dry ground appear.' And it was so" (Genesis 1:9).* First there was the Holy Spirit then there was the land or dirt.

The point is, of course, that the Holy Spirit has always existed as part of the Trinity. He did not, as some have said or written, begin His existence at Pentecost. He was there at time's beginning and He was present throughout the Old Testament era for the Old Testament quotes Him more than eighty times, each time conveying God's desire to restore and build up.

While God always exists beyond time's confines, it often helps our human understanding if we can grasp some of God's actions within the context of time. In addition to the Spirit's part in creation and the other Old Testament references to His presence, He was also the One who inspired the Old Testament's writers.

The Holy Spirit in The New Testament
"The Holy Spirit will come upon you, and the power of the Most High will overshadow you. So the holy one to be born will be called the Son of God" (Luke 1:35). These words announcing the conception of Jesus to Mary, His mother, are the beginning of the Holy Spirit's ministry in the New Testament era. His presence from that announcement to Mary until Pentecost marks a number of milestones in Christ's life. These landmark moments include Jesus' baptism when John the Baptizer saw the Holy Spirit descend like a dove. Later Christ introduced His first sermon in the synagogue by acknowledging the Spirit's presence: *"The Spirit of the Lord is on me, because he has anointed me to preach good news*

to the poor. He has sent me to proclaim freedom for the prisoners and recovery of sight for the blind, to release the oppressed, to proclaim the year of the Lord's favor" (Luke 4:18,19).

On another occasion when Jesus cast out demons the Pharisees argued that He must do so by the devil but Jesus quickly corrected that assertion and credited His healing power to the Holy Spirit. Later the writer to the Hebrews says that Christ's entire redemptive ministry was carried on in the power of the Holy Spirit: *"How much more, then, will the blood of Christ, who through the eternal Spirit offered himself unblemished to God, cleanse our consciences from acts that lead to death, so that we may serve the living God!" (Hebrews 9:14).* What a glorious Savior! What a wonderful Holy Spirit!

The Day The Power Fell
Then came Pentecost! This marked the beginning of a second era of the Holy Spirit's work which continues today and will last until the end of the world as we know it. With Pentecost the church was empowered to move beyond the land of Israel into the world: *"You will receive power when the Holy Spirit comes on you; and you will be my witnesses in Jerusalem, and in all Judea and Samaria, and to the ends of the earth" (Acts 1:8).*

There was never before a moment like it in world history, nor has there been since. People, no matter what their background, heard Peter's sermon instantly translated into their local dialect. It was like those television pictures we have seen when the United Nations is in session and each member wears an earphone that brings the spoken word in his or her own language. Because a translator stands by a microphone translating each speech the French delegate hears it in French regardless of the language of the speaker, the German delegate hears it spoken in German and so on. There were, however, no electronic earphones on Pentecost.

91

There was only God's word through God's man empowered by God's Spirit. Peter's message was instantly translated as it traveled through the air from his mouth to each listener's heart without a human translator. The Holy Spirit was the multi-lingual interpreter of the day. Even more amazing is that each person there not only heard the message in his or her national language but in his or her local dialect.

What an exciting day for church growth that was! Sinners, convicted of their sin, turned to Jesus in masses. There were 3,000 people saved one day, 5,000 the next and so forth! The church, now empowered from on high, was on the march and nothing could stop her and nothing will for Christ said, *"The gates of Hades will not overcome it" (Matthew 16:18).*

Power To The People

Today the story is the same in every church where Christ's power is sought by Christ's people. As the church advances Christ's cause in the world it does so successfully only under the guiding power of the Holy Spirit. His work will continue until the end of this age, *"'Not by might nor by power, but by my Spirit,' says the LORD Almighty" (Zechariah 4:6).*

Does not your soul soar when you realize what an amazing movement God's Holy Spirit has invited you to join? Are you not delighted to know God has chosen you to be empowered with His Holy Spirit and advance His work through you in this new day?

Our Strength: The Holy Spirit!

Recently a visiting out of town couple leaving one of our Sunday morning worship services said to me, "We come here every six weeks or so to worship because we feel the Holy Spirit's presence here." To this we respond, *Praise God from whom all blessings flow!* The Holy Spirit is still very much involved in empowering Christ's life in us.

Christ's Spirit is present in every worship service for He said, *"Where two or three come together in my name, there am I with them" (Matthew 18:20).* He heartens our singing: *"Sing and make music in your heart to the Lord" (Ephesians 5:19).* The Holy Spirit empowers our preaching: *"Our gospel came to you not simply with words, but also with power, with the Holy Spirit and with deep conviction" (1 Thessalonians 1:5).* He brings worship alive: *"For the letter kills, but the Spirit gives life" (2 Corinthians 3:6).* Worship without the Holy Spirit is dead. Worship in which the Holy Spirit is given freedom to do business for Christ is alive, vibrant and life transforming.

On Pentecost a timid, weak-kneed, frightened, confused group of direction-less disciples became dauntless, wise, strong leaders and preachers of Christ's cross, resurrection and power for living. Wherever the Holy Spirit is at work He comforts the afflicted and afflicts the comfortable.

The Holy Spirit enables our faith profession: *"No one can say, 'Jesus is Lord,' except by the Holy Spirit" (1 Corinthians 12:13).* He interprets our prayers: *"Because the Spirit intercedes for the saints in accordance with God's will" (Romans 8:27).*

The Holy Spirit empowers our work in Christ's name: *"It was he who gave some to be apostles, some to be prophets, some to be evangelists, and some to be pastors and teachers, to prepare God's people for works of service, so that the body of Christ may be built up" (Ephesians 4:11-12).*

The Holy Spirit is our teacher. He not only equips people to teach among us but He gives life to their message: *"When he, the Spirit of truth, comes, he will guide you into all truth...He will bring glory to me by taking from what is mine and making it known to you"* *(John 16:13-15).*

The Power Who Points Us To Jesus

In all these areas of our life together in the church the Holy Spirit has one aim, and only one. That aim is to point us to God's beloved Son with whom He is well pleased. The Spirit never draws attention to Himself but only to Jesus. In that alone will we find fulfillment in our relentless pursuit of excellence for Christ.

F.B. Meyer, discovered that opening his entire life to the Holy Spirit enabled him to overcome a secret sin that had dogged his life for many years. After a long battle he prayed, "Lord, here are the keys to my life. Take them and unlock every door. Fill each room and make me willing to welcome You there." In response to that prayer God's Spirit moved in and through F.B. Meyer's life as never before. In the Spirit's power he was used in ways he had not previously dreamed. His ministry spread from London all across the world. Today, more than half a century after his death, he is still touching lives through the message of his forty books, tracts and articles. His life is a splendid illustration of what God can do with any of us who open ourselves completely to Him. The same Holy Spirit will answer that prayer in each of us in ways that are exciting and good.

Does God's Holy Spirit have the keys to every room in your life? Someone asked Gypsy Smith how to start a revival in their church. "Go home," Gypsy Smith replied, "and lock yourself in your room. Kneel in the middle of the floor. Draw a chalk circle around yourself and ask God to start the revival inside that circle. When He does, the revival has started." Have you used any chalk recently?

Fort Pitt Quaker merchant and historian, James Kenny, kept good records in his diary for the earliest days of our city. For August 30, 1762, he writes about how the Holy Spirit called a young Presbyterian school teacher from Londonderry in Northern Ireland to mold a group of mixed Christians into a congregation of believers. These were ordinary men and women from every walk of life whom God had chosen to advance Christ's work across Western Pennsylvania. That was First Presbyterian Church of Pittsburgh's beginning.

As we dedicate ourselves to Christ and to working together, it will also be our present and our future. Let every heart be open, and let us spend ourselves to reach this city and the world for Christ in the power of the Holy Spirit. Working together in Him we can make a positive difference in our city and in this generation. Let revival come, O Holy Spirit, let it come quickly and let it begin in me, in Jesus' name! Amen.